Rebels or Reformers?

REBELS
or
REFORMERS?

Dissenting Priests in American Life

William Barnaby Faherty, S. J.

LOYOLA UNIVERSITY PRESS

Chicago

Loyola University Press
3441 North Ashland Avenue
Chicago, Illinois 60657

Book design by C. L. Tornatore

Library of Congress Cataloging-in-Publication Data

Faherty, William Barnaby, 1914-
Rebels or reformers? : dissenting priests in American life / by
William Barnaby Faherty.
p.   cm.
Bibliography: p.
Includes index.
ISBN 0-8294-0587-9
1. Catholic Church—United States—Clergy—Biography.
2. Dissenters, Religious—United States—Biography.   I. Title.
BX4670.F34   1988
282'.73—dc19

[B]

88-309
CIP

Dedicated to
my Jesuit colleagues
Fathers Louis A. Barth,
Lucius F. Cervantes,
John J. Killoren,
and
John M. Scott

CONTENTS

INTRODUCTION

Rooted in the spirit of independence, Americans have always been ready to question what they thought they could better. Our Bill of Rights recognizes the place and value of varying opinions, and our countrymen have always prided themselves on giving those who disagree a chance to have their say.

From the beginning of the Republic, priests have been among those who have questioned policies of both church and state. Some disagreed with a repressive law. A few complained of the lack of a needed law. Others opposed the policy of the national or state government. A few questioned a teaching of the Church, and many others questioned some policy or position of their bishop or local superior.

One clergyman criticized the Eighteenth Amendment because it restricted freedom, unlike other amendments that enlarged the scope of liberty. Several priests in one archdiocese criticized their archbishop for failure to welcome blacks. Another told that archbishop's successor, who took a lead in school integration, that he ought to volunteer to work on the African missions. The reforms of Vatican II had both supporters and critics among the clergy. Most priests have followed the authoritative position of the hierarchy. But some outstanding individuals have questioned particular attitudes or policies in a way that influenced the church and, in some instances, the nation.

In the eighteenth century, for example, Father Pierre

1

Gibault, the French-Canadian pastor of the town of Kaskaskia, would have been expected to obey his bishop and remain loyal to the Crown, because Bishop Jean-Olivier Briand of Quebec had threatened to suspend any French-Canadian priest who supported the Americans. Father Gibault, however, actively helped Colonel George Rogers Clark who led the Virginia troops in the colonists' conquest of the Old Northwest Territory, becoming thereby the first priest-dissenter in American history.

In the early national period (1820-1840), parishioners and bishops disagreed sharply over the assignment and removal of pastors in some areas. Laymen set out to exercise more control over the temporalities of their parishes, as their Protestant neighbors did. After all, they gave the money and should have some control over its use. Many of them, further, had business experience, while the seminaries offered no courses in accountancy or business administration. Sometimes individuals on both sides of the controversies acted high-handedly and even resorted to violence. An exaggerated reaction to the effort of laymen to have a greater voice in church affairs thwarted discussion and reasonable decision in the area of control of church property. Even Vatican II avoided the question of "trusteeism," as these lay efforts were called, and no individual priest has yet dominated in any controversy over "trusteeism." This remains an issue for a future generation to address fully.

In the 1840s and 1850s nativists provoked a series of attacks on the immigrant Catholics, newly arrived from Ireland and Germany, and on the schools they tried to set up. All Catholic energy went into a defense of their rights.

Individual priests in the unseceded Border States during the Civil War dissented sharply with the decision of the Lincoln administration to use force to bring the Southern states back into the Union. Many more questioned the repressive policies of Reconstruction governments that forgot President Lincoln's call to bind up the nation's wounds. The most influential of the Border State dissenters, Father John B. Bannon, a St. Louis pastor, significantly aided the Confederate cause as a chaplain in the army of the Trans-Mississippi, and even more as special agent of the Davis government to his native Ireland. Restrictive laws during Reconstruction prevented his return to his parish after the conflict.

2

The same severe anti-Confederate laws that kept Father Bannon out of the country forced all Missouri clergymen to take an oath that they had refrained from aiding the Confederate cause or even an individual Confederate in an endless variety of ways. An outstate Missouri pastor, young Father John Cummings refused to take the oath and went to jail—even though no one seemed to know whether he had been pro-Union or pro-Confederate. His case eventually went all the way to the Supreme Court and became a landmark decision in civil liberties.

In connection with civil liberties and, in particular, the right of free expression, some mention should be made of Father David Phelan, who began a Catholic paper, the *Western Watchman,* shortly after the end of the Civil War. He gradually came to see himself as the divinely appointed protector of nuns, priests, and the people against bigots and bishops. His was an independent style of journalism, unknown among Catholic priests in America in his day or today. He wrote incisively on many issues. His influence was not nationwide, but at a time when Catholic newspapers averaged about four years in duration, his *Western Watchman* continued to be a success for fifty years.

In almost every part of the country at one time or another in the years after the Civil War, individual priests protested the actions or policies of their bishop, usually on the matter of the transfer of pastors. The most famous of all dissenting pastors, Father Edward McGlynn, a social reformer of New York, disagreed with his archbishop on a far wider variety of issues than mere change of a parish. When his archbishop tried to keep him from speaking on a political issue, he spoke openly. The archbishop excommunicated him.

With the close of the frontier and the rise of manufacturing in the cities, management imposed repressive conditions—low pay, long hours, unsafe conditions, antiunion policies—on the thousands of immigrant workers who flocked to the country between 1840 and World War I. Father Cornelius O'Leary, an outstate Missouri pastor, was the first priest to support openly the cause of the Knights of Labor, America's first great labor union. He supported a major strike, testified in favor of workingmen before a congressional committee, and as a result he ran afoul of his archbishop.

After Cardinal Gibbons won Rome's approval of the

Knights of Labor and Pope Leo XIII issued the social encyclical *Rerum Novarum,* many priests took up the cause of the laboring man. Often they faced opposition in the front, the rear, and on both flanks. Only after World War I and the Great Depression did priests who supported the worker win a wide sympathetic hearing.

A number of professors of theology in American seminaries were alert to the new wave in the theological and scriptural study that swept western Europe in the early twentieth century. One of the most noted of these professors was Father Francis Duffy of the archdiocese of New York, who was to become famous during World War I as the chaplain of the "fighting Sixty-ninth." He edited a theological journal, the *New York Review.* Pope Pius X saw great danger in some of the new views. Lumping them together under the name of "modernism," the Pope issued a severe condemnation that did more than root out the evils of the movement. It squelched theological reflection and eliminated Father Duffy from the list of significant reformers.

Among the many priests who gave guidance in the field of industrial relations in the years after the Great Depression, such men as Msgr. George Higgins at the National Catholic Welfare Conference, Leo Brown in conciliation, and John Corriden "on the waterfront" regularly made the headlines. But the man who held the central position of influence during the first half of the century, was Msgr. John A. Ryan, who exerted great influence on the social reforms associated with the New Deal.

In more recent times disagreements arose over the reluctance of so many communities to move doggedly toward a fair racial policy. During the struggle for equality after World War II, Catholics took the lead in school integration in St. Louis, Missouri; Mobile, Alabama; Fort Smith, Arkansas; New Orleans, Louisiana; Wilmington, North Carolina, and other places in former slave states.

Many priests took part in promoting these racial advances. Father Claude Heithaus brought moral issues to the fore in the integration of St. Louis University, the first university in a slave state to integrate faculty and student body. Albert S. Foley made Catholics aware of the heroism of the nation's black clergy with his books *God's Men of Color* and *Bishop Healy, Beloved Outcaste.*[1] The scion of a prominent family, John La Farge, S.J. dedicated his pen and organizing skills to many causes, including race relations. While he lent prestige to the movement from his editorial office in Manhattan, three interesting and influential men manned the trenches: Father Stephen Theobald, a St. Paul pastor, the first black priest educated in an American seminary; William Markoe, also a northerner, who founded the *Interracial Review*; and Floridian Louis Twomey, who prepared an entire generation of youth, northern as well as southern, for needed change in race relations.

The most brilliant and successful dissenter in American history, the theologian John Courtney Murray, endured years of Roman silencing, only to come out during Vatican II (1962-65) as the architect of the Declaration of Religious Liberty, a landmark in Church and American Catholic history.

Priests in the field of religious sociology, such as Joseph Fichter and Andrew Greeley, offered extensive studies of Catholic practices and attitudes, and pointed the way to many avenues of reform and regularly provoked controversy.

During the 1970s, the Berrigan Brothers—Dan, a Jesuit poet, and Phil, a Josephite missionary among blacks in the South—took up the cause of peace in the Vietnam War. Frustrated by the politics of the Pentagon, they launched out in dramatic protests and for a time held the headlines. They reflected a time of social activism. After them, young Catholics interested in social reform spent their time in protests rather than in the promotion of unions, cooperatives or family farm organizations that had attracted an earlier generation of social-minded Catholics.

In the 1980s, dissenters have emerged again from among theologians; this time not in the area of dogma, scripture, or liturgy but in the area of sexual morality. Father Charles Curran, the "crown prince" of these dissenters from traditional teaching, looked upon questionable practices as acceptable in certain instances. His dissent involved many issues:

> How far did a professor's freedom of expression go? Did the greater publicity given to the theories of theologians since Vatican II add new responsibilities to their discussions? What were the limits of dissent, and the guidelines for that dissent? What did institutional loyalty require of one who chose to participate in the work of an organization? What was the special responsibility of teachers in canonically designated institutions? Why was the principle of subsidiarity, which required action on the lowest possible

5

level before allowing recourse to a higher authority, applicable in economic and political life but not in religious life? What was the full nature of the teaching body of the Church? Did it include theologians as well as bishops, and, if theologians, why not church historians, religious sociologists, and other scholars? Were not Thomas Aquinas and Peter Canisius doctors of the Church even though they were not bishops?

Even those who strongly disagreed with Curran felt that his case pointed again to the need of appropriate processes for honest doubt and for gaining a fair hearing for less popular opinions. No diocese as yet had seen the value of a "loyal opposition" or a "constructive minority." To many, the Church seemed less close to reflecting the genius of the American people than it had been at the consecration of Bishop John Carroll.

Be that as it may, Father Curran and the preceding four priests discussed here are still alive. The passage of time will allow a more objective evaluation of their work than is now possible. As for the other priests discussed in this work, they reflect various values in the history of American life and continue to offer rich lessons for their fellow Catholics. Two dissented exclusively against the state's and the local church's racial posture. One devoted himself to industrial and racial reform. Two questioned their bishop's forays into the political realm. One opposed the federal government's war on the South. Another rejected a state law that restricted his religious liberty. One defended the rights of labor. Another supported religious liberty and opposed a questionable theory of church and state that had been an endless embarrassment to American Catholics in dealing with their neighbors.

This collection of essays highlights moments in the lives of these reformers and serves mainly to bring attention to their chief accomplishments. But more remains to be told.

CHAPTER 1

PATRIOT PRIEST OF THE WEST

Pierre Gibault (1735–1802)

Father Pierre Gibault, pastor of Kaskaskia in the French-Illinois Country, had greater influence on the success of the American Revolution than any of the priests in the English colonies on the Atlantic seaboard. And in doing so he dissented from a decision of his religious superior, Bishop Jean-Olivier Briand of Quebec. The bishop had threatened to expel from the Church all French Canadians who supported the American colonies in revolt. His reasoning was plain: It was King George III who had given religious freedom to Canadian Catholics in 1774. And it was the New England Puritans who had raged against the king and the Catholic religion.

Kaskaskia is located along the Mississippi River, almost a thousand miles from Quebec. When colonial troops from Virginia and Kentucky came to French villages in Illinois, Gibault supported them in his own parish and won the people of Vincennes to their side; by so doing, he cut ties with his bishop in Quebec. Gibault's dedication to the American cause ranks him with other great patriots. He was the nation's first significant dissenting priest.[1]

The wandering missionary who was to travel throughout the central Mississippi Valley on his pastoral rounds from 1768 to 1802 was the son of a wanderer. His father moved the family regularly. Pierre was born in Montreal; his three sisters and one

brother were born in other Canadian towns. He had a good education, if one were to judge by his surviving letters. As a young
man, he went on a fur-trading expedition to the Great Lakes area
and wrote of making a journey by canoe from Detroit to Michili-
mackinac at the head of Lake Huron in 1759.[2] At some time in
his mid-twenties Pierre decided to enter the seminary. Having
completed two years of theological studies, he was ordained on
March 19, 1768 by Bishop Briand, who then assigned him to
Kaskaskia, the most important settlement in Illinois. He left Quebec for the mid-continent in June of that year.

Jesuit missionaries in the early 1700s had followed the
Kaskaskia Indians from their former homes in northern Illinois to
a site along the Kaskaskia River, just above where it emptied into
the Mississippi. It lay 120 miles above the junction of the Ohio
and the Father of Waters. Around the Indian villages, six or
seven hundred French-Canadian traders and farmers and three
hundred blacks had gathered over the years. Five companies of
the Eighteenth Royal Irish regiment, many of them Catholic, had
arrived that spring.[3] A number of Yankee traders had come by
the time of Gibault's arrival at Kaskaskia, his first parish and the
focal point of his missionary journeys.

In 1768 only one other priest served this area, which was
larger than France. He was the ex-Jesuit Father Sebastian
Meurin, pastor at Prairie du Rocher, a town near the former
French fortress of Fort Chartres about twelve miles north of
Kaskaskia. When the French government ordered the removal of
all the Jesuits from the French domains a few years before, Father
Meurin had gone to plead his case with the Council in New
Orleans. He pestered the members of that body until they gave
him permission to return to his people.

Unfortunately, the French settlements were in a state of
turmoil. The Treaty of Paris at the close of the French and Indian
War five years before, in 1763, had given the lands east of the
river to England. The settlers remembered the sad story of their
fellow French in the Province of Acadia (later Nova Scotia),
where the British troops, abetted by New England Puritans, had
uprooted all the French inhabitants, splitting and scattering families along the Atlantic coast. Feeling uneasy, the French residing
along the east bank of the river actually considered moving across
the river to territory that King Louis had given to his ally, the

8

king of Spain. These fears shared by the Illinois French were solidly grounded. Two years later, in 1770, the British government did seriously consider expelling them but wisely decided to refrain from this evil plan.

In a letter to their bishop, Father Meurin expressed his pleasure with having received Gibault as an assistant, whose zeal and energy he praised.[4] The young pastor had brought most of the parishioners back to their Easter duties. His next concern centered on the sagging log church with its leaky roof. The parishioners did not want to build a new one, but Father Gibault insisted. The result was a solid structure that was to last until 1838.

Kaskaskia was the southernmost French village in the Illinois Country. The Indian tribes to the north had been traditionally friendly, while those to the south, such as the Chickasaw, Choctaws, and Creeks had allied themselves with the British. In his first four years in the Illinois Country, hostile raiders captured Father Gibault three times during his missionary journeys. A short time after each capture, they would put him under secrecy not to reveal their whereabouts and set him free. At first he had always travelled armed, usually carrying two pistols in his belt. After the third capture, he decided his guns were too provocative and were better left at home.[5] Soon the French who travelled with him came to realize that the hostile Indians respected the priest, and his presence was regarded as better than a cavalry escort for travellers between towns. As time went on, Indians hesitated to attack a group of whites when they knew the Blackrobe was with them.

After Father Meurin's initial approval of his young colleague, he began to have misgivings about Gibault's lack of taste for study, his liking for games with the young men, and his participating in the parish festivities.[6] As a young voyageur, the agile, wiry Gibault had prided himself on his wrestling skill. No doubt he occasionally accepted a challenge even after he donned the cassock.

While Father Gibault travelled from one French village to another, baptizing infants, blessing brides and grooms, and anointing the sick, a different kind of sickness struck the Atlantic seaboard colonies, a strong distaste for British rule. The troops of His Majesty George III had traded bullets at Lexington and Concord with the colonists. The English colonies were in revolt. On May 25, 1775, Bishop Briand published an official document condemning the rebels and threatening with severe penalties any French Canadian who would support them.[7] During that summer Gibault visited Montreal and was still there in November when the American General Richard Montgomery captured the city. Gibault remained there until the spring of 1776. It is highly unlikely that he did not know of the censure that any cooperator with the Americans would incur.

During the following year (1777) Father Meurin died, leaving the entire Illinois Country to his colleague.[8] Father Gibault's territory then extended from Mackinac about 800 miles away on the northern straits to the mouth of the Arkansas River, 250 miles south of Kaskaskia. It included the settlements of Mackinac, Green Bay, Prairie du Chien, Peoria, Vincennes, Cahokia, Prairie du Rocher, and Kaskaskia. The only other priest in the midwest, the German Capuchin Bernard de Limpach, served the people of St. Louis, a new settlement on the west bank of the mighty river, about 50 miles north of Father Gibault's parish church. The east side of the stream had only Gibault.

France made an alliance with the American colonies in 1778 and prepared to renew its long-standing hostility to Great Britain. In turn, England sent Lord Charles Cornwallis with his army to harrass the southern colonies and planned a pincer movement on the Mississippi Valley. The British fortified cities along the gulf and placed troops at Baton Rouge and Natchez on the Mississippi. From the Great Lakes region to the north, they would send Indian warriors.

To counteract this threat, twenty-six-year-old Colonel George Rogers Clark led an expedition of Virginia and Kentucky militiamen into the Illinois Country. In the meantime the British had removed the Eighteenth Irish regiment. On the night of July 4, 1778, Clark's force surprised and captured the undefended town of Kaskaskia. Many villagers feared that Clark and his "Long-Knives"—as the French called the Virginians—would drive them from their homes to the far side of the Mississippi River.

Father Gibault urged the townsfolk to remain calm. He promised to confer with Clark as soon as the Virginia colonel was willing to see him. Father Gibault met with Clark a day later and won assurance that the Americans would not expel the Kaskas-kians or restrict their religious freedom. Further, Clark brought the news that France had allied itself with the colonies in revolt against England.

The priest became convinced that his people's future lay with the Americans. He urged them to support Clark. They agreed to do so. He later travelled to Vincennes on the Wabash River to win that settlement. In doing so he gained top place on the lists of enemies of the "Crown" in the book of British General Henry Hamilton. The French called Hamilton the "Hair Buyer" because he had bonuses for those who brought in French scalps. He would gladly have added Gibault's to his collection.

Historians have often asked whether or not Clark could have succeeded without French support. Since the Indians would have gone with the French, some historians think not. Clark's force was too small, too isolated, too ill-equipped. Strong Indian allies of the French lived in Southern Ohio. They could cut off Clark's path of retreat. Gibault's influence turned danger to hope. Virginia's Governor Patrick Henry thanked Father Gibault for his assistance and even suggested that the priest might help in win-ning over the people of Detroit to the American cause.

Father Gibault could stand up to Clark in their initial meeting and not hesitate to hazard the wrath of Hamilton. But he still could not face up to telling his bishop that he had become convinced of the American cause, believed the future lay with them, and had aided Clark. He had alweys been a man of hills and valleys, of strong enthusiasms and deep feelings of failure. He was on the downswing in his last letter to His Lordship. Penitently, he asked to be recalled to his diocese, but the bishop ignored his request.[9] He was to remain in Illinois.

Father Gibault continued to live for more than twenty years after the surrender of Cornwallis at Yorktown. The change in jurisdiction from the diocese of Quebec to that of Baltimore did not greatly ease the difficulties he worked under. The Illinois Country was too remote from the Atlantic seaboard colonies, and it was not well organized for some years. Footloose priests who happened to come through the area at regular intervals created additional problems for the veteran. He finally transferred to the more stable Spanish-ruled west bank of the river and served as the pastor of the town of New Madrid until his death in 1802.

A lone priest for most of the time, he had more than survived on a difficult frontier for thirty-four years. The first dissenting priest in United States history, Father Gibault was a patriot who realized that the future lay with the Americans and adopted their cause as his own.

CHAPTER 2

CONFEDERATE AGENT

John B. Bannon (1829–1913)

John B. Bannon holds a unique place in the gallery of Confederate heroes. A native of Ireland rather than of the American South, he served the Confederacy in a dual capacity; first, as chaplain of the famed First Missouri Confederate Brigade in the western theater of the war, and later as one of two special agents sent by Jefferson Davis to Ireland to plead the cause of the Confederacy.

In his capacity as chaplain, he regularly received acclaim for bravery under fire from his commanding officer, General Sterling Price, who was formerly governor of Missouri. During the siege of Vicksburg, he quieted a potential panic when Federal guns hit the church while he was saying Mass. After the surrender of Vicksburg, he went to Richmond where Confederate President Jefferson Davis asked him to return to his native Ireland to explain the position of the seceding states. He agreed to do so and ran the blockade to the Bahamas.

At the end of the war, Missouri law prevented him from returning to his parish in St. Louis, a parish he had left in the early months of the struggle. Like Confederate Secretary of State Judah Benjamin, who also was obliged to leave the States after Appomattox, Father Bannon was able to carve out a second career of distinction. He joined the Jesuit order in Ireland and became an outstanding pastor and retreat director.

In his article on Father Bannon in the *New Catholic Ency-clopedia,* published in New York in 1967, Father Aloysius F. Plaisance, O.S.B., Professor of History at St. Bernard's Abbey in Culman, Alabama, devotes thirty-one lines to his subject's American years, and only four to his second career in Ireland.[1] The writer of Father Bannon's obituary in the *Dublin Telegraph* on July 1, 1913 concentrates on his second career, dismissing his American years in a single paragraph.[2] Both aspects of his life's story deserve attention. Although the American years belong more appropriately to this study, still it is worthwhile noting that Father Bannon's willingness to begin anew, instead of wasting energy pining about the "lost cause," indicates an impressive quality of character.

The only extant portrait of John Bannon, used both in American and Irish publications, shows a tall, robust man, perhaps a little overweight at the time, who fulfills the image of the beloved and successful Irish-American monsignor. It was his service to the Confederacy—both as a chaplain who won praise from his superior officers for bravery and as an effective Confederate agent in his native land—that brought him recognition in America.

Before he was thirty, Father John B. Bannon had become pastor of St. John the Evangelist Church in St. Louis, a vital west-side parish that was predominantly Irish. There in 1858 he built a church. He was a highly intelligent man, well educated, popular, with a fine pulpit presence. To many he seemed destined for the episcopacy in the American West. Other priests in St. Louis of equal or lesser talents were so destined; so, too, was one of his cousins in Australia. But the Civil War was to play tricks with what had seemed to be his destiny.

St. Louis was a border city, generally Southern in its way of life because of its steamboat trade on the river that connected it to the interests of New Orleans and the central South. It had a number of old-line colonial French families allied by marriage to many wealthy, newcome Irish, and a number of Southern sympathizers among its Anglo-American civic leaders. It was a city free of extreme Abolitionists on the one hand and fire-eating Southerners on the other. Many reflected the attitude of General Daniel Frost, a New York-born officer and a hero of the Mexican War, who worked to build the state militia as an instrument of neutrality between the excesses of Massachusetts and those of South Carolina. Father Bannon was chaplain of a unit of the militia.

Missouri was a large and rich state that allowed slavery; but slave property was a minor factor in the state's economy. With the admission of Kansas as a free state, Missouri became a peninsula of slavery bounded by free states to the west, north, and east. It differed from other slave states in that it had a growing industrial base and a large commercial and manufacturing center, St. Louis. Missouri had taken a moderate stance in the election of 1860, giving all of its electoral votes to Democrat Stephen Douglas, the only state to do so. Lincoln received some votes in St. Louis, mostly from German-American newcomers.

Shortly after Fort Sumter fell, the state militia met for its annual encampment. The St. Louis unit, under General Daniel Frost, set up Camp Jackson about twenty blocks directly west of Father Bannon's church. One morning in May, Nathaniel Lyon, a New England captain of Federal troops at the St. Louis arsenal, mustered into service several thousand of the recently arrived German immigrants. These men surrounded the state encampment and forced the surrender of General Frost. Instead of marching the troops south and away from the large group of people who had come out to witness the events, Captain Lyon moved the prisoners through a line of people that included friends, relatives, and neighbors of the captured men. Someone in the crowd fired a shot. The recently enlisted troops of Captain Lyon responded by firing on the crowd. A number of people were killed.

During the ensuing months, Lyon himself was killed in a battle at Wilson's Creek in southwest Missouri, where Missouri and Arkansas Confederates won the day. A short time later, the Missouri Confederates won at Lexington, Missouri, without the help of Arkansas or other Confederate troops. Their opponent in that town on the Missouri River near Kansas City was a troop of Chicago Irish under Colonel James Mulligan.

When Colonel Mulligan was exchanged for General Frost, the latter and many officers and men of the state militia went south to join General Sterling Price's Missouri Confederates. Among them were some of Bannon's parishioners and other St. Louis Catholics. As a result of months of soul-searching, Father Bannon left St. Louis after Mass on Sunday, December 15, 1861 in the company of two members of prominent St. Louis Catholic families, Robert A. Bakewell and P. B. Garesche. They went to Springfield, where they were met by Generals Price and Harding, and friends Frank von Phul and William Clark Kennerly, grand-nephew of explorer William Clark. On the twenty-fifth of February, General Price assigned Father Bannon to batteries under Captain Henry Guibor and William Wade.

Father Bannon kept a diary of his wartime activities so that it is easy to follow his way as he went through the first two years of the war. During battles he stayed at the frontlines, touring hospital beds later.[3] When asked on one occasion if he was afraid during the battle, Father Bannon replied, "I am in God's keeping. His will be done."[4] General Price said of him, "I have no hesitancy in saying that the greatest soldier I ever saw was Father Bannon. In the midst of the fray he would step in and take up a fallen soldier. If he were a Catholic, he would give him the rites of the church; if a Protestant and if he so desired, he would baptize him."[5]

Father Bannon's men ultimately became part of the First Missouri Confederate Brigade, one of the most famous of all regiments, which, in the opinion of some historians of the Western theater, was better than the South's Stonewall Brigade or the Union's Iron Brigade. These soldiers soon became men without a state. The Missouri government remained in the Union. Only a rump section of the state legislature voted secession and had to withdraw from the state when the militia did. The Missouri volunteers had no uniforms until after the Vicksburg campaign. Their state could offer no promise to them at all; Missouri was in the hands of the Union Army through most of the War. The Confederates of the state had no resources at their command.

Quite interestingly, the prominent men who joined the Confederacy from St. Louis were military men like Frost or Kennerly, or lawyers like former governor Trusten Polk, or architects like General Samuel Bowen. All the businessmen remained with the Union. Company F of the First Missouri Confederate Brigade grew out of the Washington Blues, a St. Louis Irish group who had been at Jefferson City during Camp Jackson's day. They had had some military training and were being used to train outstate militia at the time of the Camp Jackson affair. Soon after the Battle of Pea Ridge, the Confederate Army of the Trans-Mississippi moved east of the river. Father Bannon was at the battle of Corinth, near Shiloh, at Fort Gibson, and at Big Black, east of Vicksburg, Mississippi.[6] During the siege of Vicksburg, the St. Louis chaplain was at the breastworks daily even though the First Missouri Confederate Brigade was held in reserve.

After the surrender at Vicksburg, the Missourians were exchanged and furloughed for two months. Father Bannon traveled to Mobile and then through Petersburg to Richmond, where he met Father Benjamin J. Keiley, later bishop of Savannah. A chaplain without a command, Father Bannon reported to Bishop John McGill of Richmond to say he would gladly perform any duties assigned to him. Subsequently, he preached at a Sunday Mass. Stephen Mallory, Confederate Secretary of the Navy, one of the worshipers, invited Bishop McGill and Father Bannon to his home. Soon after, another invitation interfered with any plans Father Bannon had already made. President Jefferson Davis requested Bannon to come to the White House of the Confederacy.

In a letter years later, Bannon wrote: "After the fall of Vicksburg, I went to Mobile and thence to Richmond with the intention of returning to Demopolis (Alabama) for the muster of the Missouri troops at the end of the two months' furlough stipulated for at Vicksburg. Until then I was content to remain and do duty in Richmond."[7] With priests needed all over the Deep South and other Southern armies in the field, it seems strange that Bannon would have gone to Richmond at the time unless he had a premonition of new work.

By 1863 the South had become convinced that, in spite of apparent superiority in personnel and training, and its regular victories over the Union Army of the Potomac, the North was constantly improving and filling the breaches in its Union ranks. Southern leaders concluded that immigration from Ireland played a great part in the North's recruitment and decided to counteract it. The Confederate government planned to send several men to Ireland as agents, preferably long residents of the country who could help to stop this flow.[8] The first agent was Lieutenant James L. Capston, a graduate of Trinity College, Dublin, a resident of Virginia, and a distinguished young Confederate officer who had offered himself voluntarily for the Secret Service.[9] President Davis asked Father Bannon to be the other man.

"The Irish mission," Bannon was to write later, "was

17

altogether unexpected and accepted only after Dr. McGill's approval and advice."[10] Supplied with fifteen hundred dollars in gold, Bannon went to Wilmington, North Carolina, ran the blockade, and landed in Halifax.[11] Arriving in Dublin in the fall of 1863, he established himself at the Angel Hotel, a popular gathering place, and gave the Southern version of the causes of the war. He emphasized the ill-treatment of Catholics in the North. Capston and Father Bannon thought initially of a circular that could be placed in the hands of possible immigrants. The first one carried a letter written by John Mitchell, an Irish patriot and Virginia editor, imploring the Irish people not to project themselves unjustly into a war against a young nation, struggling like themselves for freedom.[12]

The second release featured a letter Pope Pius IX had written the previous October to Archbishops John Hughes of New York and John M. Odin of New Orleans, begging them to use every effort to bring about a peaceful solution of the difficulties in the States.[13] Father Bannon printed this letter from the Pope in poster form and mailed twelve thousand copies, two each to every parish priest in Ireland. With the posters, Father Bannon sent a personal letter. In this letter he recalled the early history of America, comparing the revolt of the Southern states with that of the early colonies against England. The only object of the war, he said, was to allow the manufacturers in the North to enrich themselves further by plundering the farmers and planters of the South. The war was not for the restoration of the old fraternal union of the past, but a war between the materialism and infidelity of the North and the remnant of Christian civilization yet dominant in the South.

He told of the depredations of the Know-Nothings in Northern cities before the war and the rifling of churches in Missouri, Virginia, Louisiana, Mississippi, Florida, and other Southern states by Federal soldiers during the conflict. Bannon gave an extra Catholic touch to the South by speaking of the Spanish Catholics in Florida, the French Catholics in Louisiana, the Irish and English Catholic settlers of Maryland and Kentucky. In the Southern cities Catholics are welcome. "Nowhere does one hear them termed beggarly, ignorant papists, low foreigners," he insisted, "as they are invariably called in the North. It was the South that crushed Know-Nothingism in the election of 1856."[14]

During February 1864, Bannon toured Ireland, visiting many priests and lecturing on the American Civil War four times.[15] During his campaign, Bannon regularly reported by letter to Judah Benjamin, Confederate Secretary of State.

Was Bannon's campaign a success? Statistically it is hard to prove, even if immigration from Ireland lessened in 1864. Other factors, such as an economic upturn in Ireland, played their part. But certainly the feeling was strong that Bannon's views became widespread among parish priests of Ireland.

President Davis thanked Father Bannon for his services, and invited him back to the South if he found a way to get there. But by that time the blockade was so complete that he saw little chance of it.[16] When the war ended, Missouri no longer seemed a place where Father Bannon could have a productive ministry, for the laws pertaining to participants in the Confederate cause were extremely restrictive. General Frost had gone to Canada. Another Missouri General, Cavalry Commander "Joe" Shelby, had crossed the Rio Grande with his horsemen. Jefferson Davis was in prison, and Judah Benjamin, the Secretary of State with whom Father Bannon dealt directly during his work in Ireland, had left for England. Like Bannon, he too would have a distinguished second career.

The climate in Missouri was not conducive to a ministry to challenge Father Bannon's outstanding talents. One historian, writing of the experiences of the clergy in Missouri in the years immediately after the Civil War, called his book *Martyrdom in Missouri*.[17] Southern sympathizers were the victims.

Bannon might have thought of going to Australia, where his cousin was bishop of Ballarat, across the bay from Melbourne. But there is no evidence that he considered that alternative. From the noise of the battlefields and the intriguing work of special agent, he went to the seclusion of a Jesuit novitiate. Soon the master of novices had to tell him to desist from his colorful tales of his campaigns in the western theater. He would have a new, less interesting but no less high-yield apostolate in Ireland.

CHAPTER 3

THE IRONCLAD OATH

John Cummings (1840–1873)

Twenty-five year old John Cummings, two years a priest, and little known beyond the small-town Missouri parish he served, went to jail in 1865 for giving a sermon. As far as anyone knew, Father Cummings did not preach treason or violent overthrow of the government. It was not anything he said that sent him to jail but simply that he preached without taking the "ironclad oath" demanded in those tense times after the Civil War. No record remains of what he said. No one thought it significant enough to put it down in writing. Yet John Cummings stands as a reminder of the worth of the individual person and of the constitutional guarantee of freedom of speech. Three times in the last fifty years, Supreme Court Justices have recalled his case in support of human freedom.

Who was this man, John Cummings? Records do not agree on the place of his birth. The files of the cemetery where his body is buried say simply: "Missouri."[1] The hospital records say "Ireland."[2] St. Vincent's Seminary in Cape Girardeau, Missouri, where he studied between 1859 and 1863, has no record other than that he was there. The only verifiable fact of his early years is that he was born some time in 1840.

Ordained by Archbishop Peter Richard Kenrick in St. Louis in 1863, just two years before his indictment, Cummings spent the rest of that year and part of the next as assistant pastor at

21

St. Malachy's Church in St. Louis. He then accepted an assignment to Louisiana, Missouri, to begin a parish for Irish immigrants.

A small, impetuous man who, in the opinion of a contemporary, looked no more than twenty-five years old,[3] Cummings
was a relatively insignificant newcomer in the old, but influential
community of Louisiana, Missouri. This largest and oldest city in
Pike County, one of the four original counties of the state, held a
prominent site on the Mississippi River, eighty miles northwest
of St. Louis and twenty-five miles below Hannibal, the town
Mark Twain would soon make famous as the home of Tom
Sawyer and Huck Finn. Pike belonged to a curving stretch of
counties along the upper Mississippi and lower Missouri rivers
that bore the name "Little Dixie." This area included many
slaveholding families and had been the residence of a dispropor-
tionate number of pre-Civil War governors of the state. Missouri,
incidentally, had not yet abolished slavery when Cummings came
to Pike County.

The region had many open sympathizers with the Confederate cause. Some men in Pike County stood at odds with the
Union. But Father Cummings did not put on record his own
views on the slavery issue that divided the nation.

Several priests of the St. Louis archdiocese had strongly
advocated states' rights, and thus had to leave Missouri during
the conflict. To avoid difficulty with Federal authorities, Father
John O'Sullivan of St. Malachy's Church in St. Louis had gone
to a less tense parish in Illinois shortly before Father Cummings
arrived at St. Malachy's for his first priestly assignment. Jesuit
Father Frederick P. Garesche so strongly preached for secession—even though his brother, Colonel Julius Garesche, died in
the Tennessee campaign of the Union Army—that he had to go to
Texas to continue his ministry during the war. Father John Bannon would not return to the United States from Ireland because of
the same oath that threatened Father Cummings.

Father Cummings, on the other hand, a totally obscure
young priest, had no conflict with Federal authorities. At one
moment in his short life he had a chance to stand up for religious
liberty and for the rights of the individual, rights that were guar-
anteed to all American citizens. He took his stand.

To understand how Missouri could make a law that

brought defiance from a man like Father Cummings, it is necessary to take a look at the earlier history of the state. Missouri was
the largest state west of the Mississippi, and it had 115,000
slaves. But slavery was a declining factor in its economy by the
midcentury. In the election of 1860, Missouri stood for modera-
tion and gave all its electoral votes to Senator Stephen A. Douglas of Illinois. It was the only state to do so. Even strong
slaveholding rural counties rejected John C. Breckinridge, the
candidate of the Deep South. Once the Gulf states seceded, however, many Missourians, including Governor Claiborne Fox
Jackson, wanted to follow them out of the Union. Strong action
by General Nathaniel Lyon, the political leadership of Francis
Preston Blair, Jr., and the militancy of the German immigrants in
St. Louis kept Missouri in the Union.

But the state became a battlefield. Accustomed as most
Americans are to think of the Civil War as a struggle fought
mainly in Virginia, they are unaware that over one thousand
engagements, battles, and skirmishes took place in Missouri.
Moreover, Missouri gave sixty percent of its men of military age
to the two armies, the highest percentage in the nation. There
were 109,000 fighting men in the Union Army and 30,000 in the
Confederate Army.[4] Because these soldiers were neighbors,
sometimes relatives, a not-unexpected bitterness gripped the
state. Furthermore, in an effort to keep Missouri in the Union and
to prevent recruits from joining the Confederate Army, the Federal, and later the State, authorities used tactics not unlike those of
a police state.

Early in 1861, the year the war broke out, politicians
demanded a loyalty oath of state officeholders and of former
Confederates wishing amnesty.[5] The next year the state authorities extended the loyalty oath to all voters, jurymen, attorneys,
and ministers of marriage ceremonies. As the war went on and
the Union forces prevailed, this oath degenerated from a touch-
stone of loyalty to a cornerstone of tyranny.

Missouri called a Constitutional Convention in 1865 under the leadership of a St. Louis lawyer, Charles Drake, a
"Know-Nothing" in the fifties, a Democrat linked with secessionists Governor C. F. Jackson and General Sterling Price in
1860, but a radical Republican in 1865. Two years later Drake's
supporters were to elect him to the United States Senate. He and

his men drew up an entirely unreasonable constitution that some described as "the Draconian Code." A loyalty oath, required by Article 2, Section 3, demanded a denial of 86 specific acts that stretched from outright treason all the way to "feeling sympathy" for the Confederate cause or for anyone involved in that cause, or for "admitting dissatisfaction with the government of the United States."[6]

At the ratification of the Constitution, Archbishop Peter Richard Kenrick of St. Louis sent a letter to all the priests in his diocese, which was then coterminus with the state, advising them not to take the oath because it seemed to require a sacrifice of religious liberty.[7] The archbishop hoped that civil officials would not enforce the law, but in the event that they did, the priests should let him know of their particular circumstances so that he could give them counsel and assistance.[8]

Peter Richard Kenrick, the first archbishop of the Trans-Mississippi United States, had been a formidable figure for many years. An immigrant himself, he had cared for the needs of the immigrants by promoting a people's bank much like a modern credit union. By dexterous handling of business affairs, he had paid the debts on the beautiful riverfront cathedral. He had written books that gave him a reputation as a minor theologian. During the course of the Civil War, he had recognized the diverse sentiments of his people and had assumed a posture of Olympian neutrality. He sent his priests to help the sick and wounded whether they wore blue uniforms or grey. Up until 1863 his brother, Archbishop Francis Patrick Kenrick, was archbishop of Baltimore, the oldest and most important diocese in the country. In short, Archbishop Kenrick was a man to reckon with, and his support gave strength to both the Catholic and Protestant clergy.[9]

Under the provisions of the "ironclad" oath, Saturday, September 2, 1865, was the last day of grace that John Cummings enjoyed. Since he had not taken the oath of loyalty, he had to make up his mind whether or not he would preach to his few Irish parishioners at Sunday Mass, or for the moment simply offer Mass without any explanation of the Gospel that was a normal part of the Sunday service. John Cummings chose to preach. Unfortunately, we have no record of this important sermon. It was not *what* he said, however, that mattered on this occasion, but that he spoke.

Archbishop Kenrick and many others in Missouri presumed that the oath would not be enforced. This did not prove to be so. A grand jury at the county seat of Bowling Green, twelve miles west of Louisiana, Missouri, indicted John Cummings on Tuesday, September 5, for his "crime." On Friday, the authorities arrested him and brought him to Bowling Green for arraignment before Judge Thomas Jefferson Fagg, a slaveholder in 1860, and a radical Republican by 1865.[10]

Cummings was not the first priest arraigned. Authorities had arrested Father Patrick Cronin, the pastor in Hannibal, Missouri, the same day they had indicted Cummings. Father John Hogan, a well-known outstate Missouri pastor who was later to become bishop of St. Joseph, Missouri, gave a colorful account of his arrest at Chillicothe, Missouri, in his book *On the Mission in Missouri*.[11] Those arrested before Cummings posted bond. The circuit judges, anxious to let the threatening storm blow over, postponed the trials until the next term of the court. But Cummings refused to seek a delay. He asked for an immediate trial and forced the hand of Judge Fagg, who had expected a postponement. The judge did not even have a court house, for fire had ravaged the Pike County Court House the year before. So the judge held court in a Methodist Church.

On the first day of the trial, Friday, September 8, 1865, John Cummings tried to act as his own counsel. When the clerk read the indictment, Cummings pleaded. "Guilty, Sir." This upset the court.

Judge Fagg paused in confusion, then informed the defendant that if this were his plea, it remained only to pronounce sentence. Fagg inquired if the prisoner had anything to say. Apparently Cummings had waited for this moment. He addressed the court in what the *Missouri Republican* called "a religious stump speech, entirely proper in itself, but not entirely pertinent to the occasion."[12] He compared his trial to that of Jesus Christ. He denounced the idea that the State had authority to interfere with his divine mission to preach. He defended the Catholic Church as the friend of the Republic by listing the outstanding Catholic officers in the Revolution and the Civil War. Finally he declared that although he had done what the indictment charged, it was patently false that he violated any just or rightful law.

U.S. Senator John Brooks Henderson, a former Democrat

now leaning toward the radical Republican position, happened to be in court that morning. He asked that Cummings be allowed to change his plea to not guilty, since his declaration of not having violated a rightful law amounted to such a plea. Judge Fagg denied the request.

In a forty-five minute "hotch-potch strain of law, politics and religion,"[13] the Senator lectured the priest for the clumsy way he had handled his case. Henderson claimed, among other things, that it was actually a heresy of the Methodist Episcopal Church South to say that the state had no authority over the ministers of religion. He assured the priest that his sympathy for the Catholic religion was as great as the priest's own; and as a sign of his good will he offered to defend Cummings in this present instance.

Newspapers of the time editorialized that Henderson knew it would be politically damaging to himself and to the radical Republicans if the priest went to jail.[14]

Cummings declined Henderson's offer. Instead, he accepted the services of a lawyer who differed sharply with the senator. Young and popular Robert Alexander Campbell, the son of a prominent Presbyterian clergyman, had served during the war as a junior officer under Henderson, then a general of militia, but opposed the radical politics of his superior. The first day in court ended with Cummings's accepting Campbell as his counsel and Judge Fagg's agreeing to a non-guilty plea.

Father Cummings spent the night in jail. According to one report, his companion for the evening was a horse thief.[15] A newspaper, however, said he shared the jail with two burglars and a rapist.[16]

The second day of the trial was brief, colorless, and predictable. The defendant admitted the facts laid down in the indictment. The judge found him guilty because he had acted as a priest and minister of the Catholic "persuasion" without having first taken, subscribed, and filed the oath of loyalty.[17] Sentenced to pay a fine of five hundred dollars and stand committed until the fine was paid, Cummings refused to pay the fine or to allow his friends to pay. He entered the county jail on Saturday.

Speaker of the House Champ Clark, a famous Pike County resident, recalled that on the next day Father Cummings's parishioners came up to Bowling Green from Louisiana. They spent most of the day camped around the cell of their pastor,[18] and scared the town fathers more than "Bloody Bill" Anderson's Confederate raiders did during the war when they stormed through central Missouri.

Father Cummings stayed in jail exactly one week. It took that long for newspapers in New York to look with shame on the events in Missouri.[19] Cummings had become a rallying point for the opponents of the Missouri Constitution and had enlisted public sympathy by focusing national attention on Missouri's loyalty oath. After the week had passed, Cummings's lawyers asked if an appeal might be made to the Supreme Court. When the court granted the request, Cummings accepted an offer of bail from Protestant friends, rather than from Archbishop Kenrick.[20]

The radical newspaper of Louisiana headlined the story of this action: "More Sensible," and made the comment: "The friends of law and order can congratulate themselves that at least in 'Old Pike' no man, no matter what his calling, is above the law."[21] On the following Monday, Cummings took a steamboat down the Mississippi to St. Louis to visit the Archbishop and a few friends.[22]

Reaction throughout the state to the news of the "rebellious priest" was spontaneous, but by no means uniform. The supporters of the Drake Constitution firmly demanded enforcement of the Test Oath Law. Opponents of the radical Republicans and church members of all denominations bitterly condemned the new constitution and approved Cummings's action. The case became a trial of the extremist policies of the radical Republicans. Appropriately, Francis P. Blair, Jr. and the German-American leaders of St. Louis, who had done so much to save St. Louis and Missouri for the Union, bitterly opposed the extremists in their own Republican party.

The technicalities of the trial before the Missouri Supreme Court have little lasting importance or interest. While the trial progressed, during the two middle weeks of October 1865, several St. Louis papers speculated that the Missouri Supreme Court might repudiate the test oath.[23] But this did not happen. Few people expected the judges to make an impartial decision. They had received their appointments under the Drake Constitution, and now they would support it. They upheld the decision of the lower court.

Early in November, Father Cummings went to St. Louis to make an appeal to a higher court. On his steamboat journey back to Pike County, he happened to meet Francis P. Blair, Jr., who was on his way to Hannibal to attack the radical constitution in a public address.[24] Blair had much at stake in the Cummings case. He had been instrumental in organizing opposition to the secessionists in Missouri, and then he had served as Major General under Sherman. Now he saw the work of five years brought to an inglorious conclusion by extremists of his own party. As a result, he volunteered to ask his brother, the able lawyer Montgomery Blair, once a member of Lincoln's cabinet, who was at the time trying to rebuild his political position in Maryland, to represent Father Cummings before the U.S. Supreme Court. Cummings accepted the offer on the spot. Blair wrote his brother, asking him to take the case without fee. He pointed out the political wisdom of doing so because of the popularity of the case with Conservatives and "the large number of Catholics in Maryland."[25] Montgomery Blair sought the aid of another outstanding lawyer, David Dudley Field, a brother both of Cyrus Field, of transatlantic cable fame, and of Stephen Field, an associate justice of the Supreme Court. Field had great concern for the issues at stake. Blair also got the advice and help of Senator Reverdy Johnson, a Maryland lawyer who had been active in the cases of Mrs. Suratt and of Dred Scott.

These distinguished counsellors offered two main arguments in behalf of Father Cummings before the Supreme Court between March 15 and 20, 1866. First, the Missouri Constitution was *ex post facto* because it defined as criminal, acts that were not criminal at the time of commission; and secondly, it assumed that all clergymen were guilty of treason and required them to prove their innocence. Thus it was "a bill of attainder" prohibited by the Constitution of the United States.[26]

The lawyers for Missouri were George Strong of St. Louis and Senator John B. Henderson, who followed the case from its first day in the Methodist Church in Bowling Green to its final resolution in the chambers of the Supreme Court. The Court waited ten months before giving its opinion on January 14, 1867. Justice Field delivered the opinion of the Court and reversed the judgment of the Missouri Supreme Court in a five to four decision.

The radical Reconstructionists in Congress did not take the decision lightly. They tended to harass Judge Field, the only Lincoln appointee to vote with the majority in the Cummings decision. The other four justices of the majority had served on the Court at the time of the Dred Scott decision ten years before.

In the meantime, Archbishop Kenrick had moved Father Cummings to St. Stephen's Parish, Indian Creek, Missouri, a rural community forty miles inland from the Mississippi River. He continued as pastor of St. Stephen's at Indian Creek until September 1870, when he became ill. He died three years later in a St. Louis Hospital. The medical records indicate no connection between his final illness and the tensions of the trial.

The story of John Cummings, then, attests the supreme worth of the individual. This impetuous little man was not a person of greatness. He left no word of wisdom by which we might remember him. He achieved little enough during his short years in his chosen profession. He did only one thing that merits our remembrance and our gratitude. He stood up for his rights as a free human being when the state tried to infringe on those rights. He spoke one Sunday morning in September 1865. He went to jail for thus speaking. He was not satisfied to bide his time, to accept a compromise, and to let things work themselves out. If the law said he could not preach, then the law was wrong and the state must repeal the law.

When Cummings died a few years later, no local newspaper, religious or secular, ran an obituary of his short life. But he left his own obituary, written in the records of the Supreme Court of the United States. The Cummings case, to quote a modern justice, stands as "one more of the Constitution's great guarantees of individual liberty."[27]

CHAPTER 4

THE KNIGHTS OF LABOR

Cornelius O'Leary (1850–1917)

Writing before the Great Depression stirred our social consciousness, an historian of the St. Louis Archdiocese claimed that Father Cornelius O'Leary's lack of prudence, his quick caustic wit, and his habit of criticism limited his priestly effectiveness.[1] Twenty years later historian Henry J. Browne ranked O'Leary among the few priest-heroes in the cause of social justice in the 1880s.[2]

The story of the Irish-born pastor and the Knights of Labor shows what happens when a learned thirty-six-year-old priest, who is an authority on canon law, a vigorous writer, and a colorful orator runs afoul of his ecclesiastical superior.

Father O'Leary had already become recognized as a strong personality when in his mid-twenties he had taken part in a religious controversy promoted by the editor of the *St. Louis Globe Democrat*.[3] He could write learnedly and objectively, or caustically and subjectively, on or off the point with equal fluency. His photo shows a challenging face with a strong jaw and the physique of a Notre Dame halfback. His superior was the redoubtable eighty-year-old Archbishop Peter Richard Kenrick, opponent of papal infallibility, often referred to as the "lion of the West."

The Noble Order of the Knights of Labor, America's first great labor union, began in 1869 as a secret fraternal organization to encompass all workers, skilled and unskilled, black and white, native-born and foreign. Secrecy would shield the workers from the "blacklists" of employers and the indiscretions of individual members. The fraternal ritual corresponded to the spirit of the times. While the specialized craft unions, by way of contrast, concentrated exclusively on gains for the skilled workers in wages and working conditions, the more visionary Knights of Labor tried to rally all workers into one large union that would give the working class a solidarity. They saw a destiny for labor to lead the country into a wide range of social reforms.

The outstanding leader of the Knights of Labor, Terence V. Powderly, a skilled worker himself, became "Grand Master Workman" or chief officer of the union in 1878. Elected mayor of Scranton on the labor ticket the same year, this mild, diplomatic, sensitive Catholic layman tried to please the general public as well as labor. By 1886, the union claimed seven hundred thousand men under his direction.

Though Powderly was a devout Catholic, his program did not please Archbishop Elzear Taschereau of Quebec, who had condemned the Knights in a message to Roman authorities. In a response dated August 27, 1883, the Holy Office denounced the Knights of Labor as a prohibited society. Archbishop John Joseph Lynch of Toronto, on the other hand, took a much more favorable view of the Knights and expressed concern for the mistreated workers in many places on both sides of the border.[4] Archbishop James Gibbons, to be named a cardinal in 1886, supported a streetcar strike that same year in Baltimore and urged his fellow bishops to follow a benevolent policy toward the laboring man.[5]

In the meantime, railroad workers out West had struck against the Jay Gould system. A first strike had occurred in the previous March (1885) when several thousand workmen of the Missouri-Pacific in the states of Missouri, Texas, and Kansas demanded a restoration of wages. The wage cut, coming without warning or justification at a time when company earnings had remained high, outraged the general public, which was already hostile to Jay Gould. The governors of Missouri and Kansas moved to end the strike. The rail officials had the good sense to yield.

In March 1886, a greater strike began. Nine thousand

shopmen struck. They not only quit work, but they set out to stop all freight traffic in a five-state area by removing small but essential mechanisms from the engines. The workers had few here-and-now demands. Their main concern was union recognition. Thus the strike became a power struggle.

Father Cornelius O'Leary, pastor of St. Rose of Lima Church in De Soto, Missouri, where the Missouri-Pacific Railroad had one of its largest shops, was away when the strike broke out on March 6. Many of the strikers were among the best members of his parish. They had just built a new stone church and paid two-thirds of the debt on it through their own contributions and proceeds from a series of lectures that Father O'Leary had given. When O'Leary returned from New York and found the strike in progress, he did not take sides immediately. He studied the situation. He found wages inadequate at best and employment spasmodic for many men during much of the year. The company hired strikebreakers, many of whom O'Leary believed to be "fit for the penitentiary." He saw each little disturbance arising from the strike magnified beyond proportion; while in the previous year ten murders had occurred in the vicinity with "no stir about it."[6] On the last day of March, Father O'Leary addressed a public meeting of all citizens on the strike.

Rumors spread through De Soto that the Missouri-Pacific would move its shops,[7] and that former employees would get their jobs back only "as individuals." They, presumably, would have to give up membership in the Knights.[8] General distress marked the plight of the strikers and their families. No credit was available.

O'Leary organized a committee of five for relief work among the poor families. He prevailed upon lawyer Richard Graham Frost, a former member of Congress and a scion of several distinguished St. Louis families, to defend indicted railroad workers. "Through his (Frost's) influence," O'Leary wrote, "the Company and the Court (practically one and the same) seemed to relax their rigor by letting them off very easily."[9]

The strike had forced business to a standstill. As a result of a coal shortage, factories had to close. Food no longer reached the family table. The general public began to reassess the struggle. Then in early April violence broke out.[10] People did not ask who committed the violence. Both sides had done their share.

But the public blamed all trouble on the walkout, and they wanted it to end. Thus, with the aid of the public authorities, the railroad company was able to crush the strike. The Knights met a decisive defeat.

With the strike already doomed to failure, the House of Representatives sent a committee to investigate labor troubles "in the Southwest." Three men made up the committee: Andrew J. Curtin, governor of Pennsylvania during the Civil War; John W. Stewart, one-term governor of Vermont; and James N. Burnes, a former judge and president of the Missouri Valley Railroad. They began hearings on April 20. While no other Catholic clergyman spoke in behalf of the workers, Father O'Leary testified on May 12.[11]

O'Leary explained his concern for the working man; described how company policies goaded the men to violence; stated his belief that some corporations wielded a power that overshadowed state and federal authorities; gave evidence of gross inequities in pay scales; condemned the use of gunmen as strikebreakers; and denounced the "blacklist."[12] Throughout his testimony, O'Leary never took a neutral posture but defended the Knights of Labor in all their actions and policies. At times he spoke excessively. Yet a careful perusal of the entire report leads the objective observer to the conclusion that O'Leary acquitted himself well, at times brilliantly, and performed a significant service to the public and the cause of justice.

Rumors made the rounds that the Missouri-Pacific would move its shops. Loyal union men could find no work in De Soto; many people moved away, business declined, and property values dropped dramatically.[13] The Records of Father O'Leary's church stated that the strike dispersed the congregation, crippled the resources of the parish, and almost ruined the town.[14] Ill-feeling and discouragement gripped De Soto.

During the summer, a representative of Pope Leo XIII, Monsignor Germano Straniero, visited St. Louis on a tour of the United States.[15] Straniero had no official capacity, except to bring to Archbishop James Gibbons of Baltimore the symbols of his new dignity as a cardinal. The remainder of his tour was simply "sight-seeing." But O'Leary took the opportunity of talking to him about the Knights of Labor. He presented the Italian prelate with documents explaining the nature and work of the order.[16] On the gangplank before reembarking for Europe a few months later, Straniero gave an interview favorable to the Knights. He said that membership in the Knights of Labor was compatible with good Catholicism and claimed few American bishops were really hostile to it.[17] The story made the rounds of the press and elicited from O'Leary an admission that he had met with the Italian prelate.[18]

At this time, Grand Master Powderly wrote:

> I have heard that the Missouri-Pacific Company has offered to build a church in De Soto, if you are removed. Is that true? If it is, I will bend every energy of mine to the building of a church for Father O'Leary and keep him just where he is. At any rate you should have a church and if you will consent to it I will start the ball a rolling that will put one up for you. Let me know your wishes. . . . [19]

In his large, free-flowing script, O'Leary thanked Powderly for his generous offer of help for a new church. He had already built a fine stone church. He admitted that he was perhaps overzealous in that his parishioners were "tenants at will, so to speak." The church still had a debt of four thousand dollars and the parish could not even pay the interest. He appreciated Powderly's offer of help, but could not consent to it. He felt it might establish a bad precedent.[20]

O'Leary had heard the rumor that the railroad officials offered to pay the debt if he were removed, and a contrary rumor among Catholics that he would *not* be removed precisely because the debt existed. The railroad officials had encouraged a petition for his removal, O'Leary stated, discharged a friend of his simply because of the friendship, threatened to move the shops on his account, and turned many citizens against him.[21]

While Father O'Leary was speaking out in defense of the Knights, many churchmen discussed the matter privately among themselves. For instance, in Philadelphia the new archbishop, Patrick Ryan, supported the Knights. "The matter becomes of very grave importance," Ryan wrote, "in view of the very great labor *contra* capital movement in the country. The Knights of Labor are in some places almost exclusively Catholic."[22]

Archbishop Kenrick, presumably, would support the

Knights. Rome had condemned them in French Canada; and Kenrick usually opposed the overcentralizing tendencies of the Roman Curia. But he had misgivings about the boycott and the tampering with the rolling stock.[23] Most surprisingly, he visited French Canada for two weeks in late summer as a guest of Cardinal Taschereau,[24] who had opposed the Knights. After returning from Canada, Kenrick had another crucial interview—this one a two-hour meeting with rail executive H. M. Hoxie. Father O'Leary, incidentally, blamed Kenrick's negative stand on this meeting.[25]

The only other archbishop who opposed the Knights, John Baptist Salpointe of Santa Fe, probably never met a labor union member in his life. He visited Kenrick on his way east to the bishop's meeting, and many blamed Salpointe's negative stand on this visit.[26]

With Kenrick and Salpointe in opposition to the Knights, and several other archbishops preferring to let Rome decide the matter, Cardinal Gibbons could not win unanimous approval of the order at the fall archiepiscopal conference. Rome would have to decide the issue.

O'Leary's work in De Soto, however, soon ended. Kenrick appointed him to a newly forming parish in a suburb of St. Louis called Webster (later Webster Groves). O'Leary believed that three factors caused his transfer: his criticism of Kenrick's conferring with railroad executive H. M. Hoxie, his support of the Knights, and his testifying before the Curtin Committee.[27] O'Leary's successor at the parish in De Soto, Father Joseph Connolly, later vicar-general of the archdiocese of St. Louis, wrote in the parish history:

> In March 1886, the strike on the railroad and in the shops, known as the "Southwestern Strike of 1886," occurred . . . forcing, as a result of the part taken in siding with the Knights of Labor, and utterances in public and private, the departure of Father O'Leary in November 1886.[28]

In the letter to Powderly of January 23, O'Leary spoke of his friendliness for Father Edward McGlynn, who had run into trouble with Archbishop Michael Corrigan of New York because of his support of Henry George's social theories and political campaign in New York. A few months later, the *New York Sun* featured an article that compared O'Leary's story with that of Father McGlynn in the East.[29]

As an expression of his appreciation to O'Leary for the debts he had incurred in assisting the striking railroad men, Powderly sent him a check for four hundred dollars as a start in paying the debt and asked him to become a regular contributor to the *Journal of United Labor*.[30] Two months later Father O'Leary and Powderly met in Philadelphia. Not long afterward Powderly asked the priest to serve as intermediary in carrying a letter of gratitude from the Knights to Cardinal Gibbons. Powderly thanked Gibbons and praised O'Leary in this letter.

No one, the Grand Master Workman wrote, rendered the cause of law and order more effectual service at that time than Father O'Leary who proved himself indeed to be the true priest of the people. "I thank Father O'Leary more than any living man for the termination of the strike before violence was resorted to.[31]

Powderly also asked Cardinal Gibbons to use his influence in behalf of the priest.[32] No evidence exists that Cardinal Gibbons attempted to intercede with Kenrick in behalf of O'Leary. Perhaps he felt that if Pope Pius IX had not budged Kenrick on another issue, he had little hope in this. But Gibbons did plead the cause of the Knights of Labor in Rome during 1887. And though he won only grudging approval, he was able to meet with Powderly and win from him agreement to Rome's few conditions. So that by the time the report of Rome's approval came out, it proved a prestigious victory for the cardinal and the Knights.[33]

Father O'Leary took a leave of absence and visited his native Ireland. There he "avowed that he was a socialist and rebel at heart, as was every Irishman."[34]

After his return to St. Louis, he wrote to Powderly in June 1888: "My friends here have corrected their errors and I forgive them."[35] He was to serve spasmodically as assistant pastor at various parishes during the nineties. After the turn of the century, the newly appointed Archbishop John J. Glennon commissioned him to develop a suburban parish, Notre Dame, in Wellston, Missouri. This work consumed his remaining years. He took no further part in domestic struggles for social justice, though he did continue to plead the cause of Ireland. Quite surprisingly,

O'Leary died as a result of injuries received when a tornado struck the railroad station in Mineral Point, Missouri, where he and a number of priests waited for a Missouri-Pacific train.

In his memoirs, *The Pathways I Trod,* Terence Powderly called in question the lack of involvement of most clergymen during the struggle of the Knights. Powderly listed the names of several bishops and many priests who supported the Knights *after* Cardinal Gibbons returned from Rome with an approval of the order in 1887. Before that, Powderly mentioned the name of only one Catholic pastor who stood up publicly for justice for the Knights of Labor, Father Cornelius O'Leary of Missouri. This is Powderly's tribute: "No man in or out of the organization did greater service to the men than Father O'Leary."[36]

This was no little achievement.

CHAPTER 5

THE WAR ON POVERTY

Edward McGlynn (1837–1900)

Back in the 1880s, an enterprising editor could have carried a photograph of two clerics under the caption: "Recalcitrant Priest and Long-suffering Bishop." The picture would have shown one as being a nervous man with an unsure gaze, a pursed mouth, and a non-paternal look, in spite of his otherwise reasonably nice features; the other would have appeared to be a handsome, slightly challenging man, with clear eyes, a fine nose, and level mouth. Surprisingly, the rebel priest would have been the latter and the beleaguered archbishop, the former. Towards the close of his life, photographs showed Doctor—he used that title rather than Father—Edward McGlynn graying but still handsome, a little weather-beaten from the long campaigns he had waged, but with a look of confidence in his eyes, which showed he was sure of his love for God and God's love for him.

At his ordination in 1860 at the basilica of St. John Lateran in Rome, people might have predicted that Edward McGlynn would become one of the outstanding members of the American hierarchy. Instead, he took antiestablishment positions on church-state matters, and his concern for the poor won him over to views on social reform that did not sit well with successive archbishops. This brought on many years of ecclesiastical feuding. McGlynn espoused the economic theories of Henry George and publicly campaigned when George ran for mayor of New York City. As a result, McGlynn ended up excommunicated; and he remained so for five years, until America's first Apostolic Delegate arrived in this country and restored him to honor. But by that time his most creative years had passed.

Edward McGlynn was one of eleven children of an East Side Manhattan family. His father died when he was ten but left the family in fairly comfortable circumstances. Edward had a good education at the 13th Street Grammar School and at the Free Academy, later to become the College of the City of New York. He graduated at the age of nineteen, a strong young man, fond of sports, reserved, but the center of any gathering once he got there. He went to Rome for ecclesiastical studies and became a priest on March 24, 1860. The outstanding American in his class, in the opinion of Irish contemporaries, he received his doctorate at twenty-three and then served as vice-rector of The American College when it was established under Father Bernard Smith, an Irish Benedictine.

At the conclusion of Smith's term, "Doctor" McGlynn went back to New York and served as an assistant to Father Thomas Farrell of St. Joseph's Church on Sixth Avenue. Farrell vigorously opposed slavery; he supported President Lincoln with enthusiasm and no doubt influenced his young assistant to study social questions. McGlynn served at several other parishes and, for a time at the end of the Civil War, as chaplain in a military hospital. At the age of twenty-nine, he returned as pastor to his native parish, that of St. Stephen's on Manhattan's East Side, then one of the most populous parishes in the country. St. Stephen's brought McGlynn face-to-face with the problems of unemployment and its attendant difficulties. He became aware of the many people who came to him seeking job opportunities, not handouts. This experience reconfirmed his interest in social questions.

McGlynn was not a man to follow the crowd. At a time when interfaith cooperation was minimal, he fraternized with clergy of other denominations. He helped Jewish institutions. In a *New York Sun* interview of April 30, 1870, he strongly supported the public schools, looking on them as the safeguard of American institutions. He called for an amendment to the state constitution that would (1) forbid appropriations of school funds to any but common schools; (2) outlaw prayers, Bible reading, or any distinctly religious activity in the common schools; (3) end the appointment of chaplains to state institutions; (4) repeal all arrangements of cooperation between the state and religious bodies in the field of health, education or welfare; and (5)—the one positive platform —encourage the visits of clergymen and other citizens of all denominations to public institutions.[1] In short, he would have eliminated all but the minimal cooperation of church and state in the areas of health, education, and welfare.

McGlynn had a brilliant mind, but he was not an exact student, and he did not read widely. Like so many personable and naturally talkative Irish-Americans, he relied on personal charm rather than on penetrating scholarly analysis to win a point. But he became acquainted with the theories of the American craftsman-turned reformer, Henry George, who had become convinced of the unsoundness of the capitalistic system. George saw the wealthy grow richer and the poor more destitute and dependent. With this in mind, George worked out a thesis with land and its possession as the key. He contended that people were entitled to a fair share of land in the same way they were entitled to water and air. Any system that denied them access to the land was undemocratic.

In order to lessen and eventually eliminate the inequities of landholding, George proposed a land tax adjusted in such a way that the gain, or what he termed the "unearned increment," coming by reason of location and civic growth, would go to the community as a whole. To the young reformer, economic rent was a form of robbery. By virtue of having to pay such rent, all elements of society received less return from their labors than was their due. George would, therefore, have siphoned off this economic rent in taxation and then abolished all other forms of contribution to the government. In the end, the single tax would, in his judgment, allow the government to take over the railroads and telegraphs and inaugurate a vast program of social services for the general public. George expounded these views in 1879 in a book entitled *Progress and Poverty*. Few people could honestly question George's condemnation of evils. Many, however, thought some of his schemes impractical. Furthermore, his insistence that land belonged in some way to all men frightened people at a time when extreme socialism threatened many horizons.

Ideas such as these had appeared in England. No doubt

41

George borrowed from his English forerunners. But his book gave American readers the first opportunity to learn of the promising theories of the single tax. His program was simple. His book enjoyed a tremendous vogue.

When George sailed for Ireland in October 1881, as a correspondent of the *Irish World* of New York, he carried his campaign to a country that had a vexing land question. George's affiliation with the Irish Land Leaguers brought him into contact with Irish agitators such as Michael Davitt. Since so many Catholic bishops and priests in the United States were of Irish ancestry and thus deeply concerned over the settlement of the Irish land question, they became aware of Henry George and his theories.

When Michael Davitt arrived in the United States in August 1882, Doctor McGlynn gave public expression to his views on the single tax at a meeting in behalf of the Irish Land Leaguers. Without reservation, McGlynn espoused the teaching of George as a solution for the ills of the masses in the United States as well as in Ireland. Rome heard of McGlynn's speech. Giovanni Cardinal Simeoni, Prefect of the Propaganda, the Roman agency that took care of the Church in such out-of-the-way mission countries as the United States, Indo-China, and Zanzibar, sent word to McGlynn's superior, John Cardinal McCloskey, stating that the priest's utterance on the rights of property were socialistic in character. Simeoni demanded that the Cardinal reprimand McGlynn and if necessary, suspend him. McCloskey conferred with McGlynn and won a promise that he would make no more public speeches on the subject. There the matter rested for three years until the death of the Cardinal.

When McCloskey died in October 1885, McGlynn presumed that since his promise had been a personal one, it no longer held.[2] In the following autumn, Henry George ran for the office of mayor of New York. McGlynn agreed to address a rally of the Labor Party on October 1, backing the George candidacy. The new archbishop, Michael Corrigan, formerly of Newark and a fellow student with McGlynn in Rome, forbade him to do so. The priest refused to keep silent. As a consequence, on the next day Corrigan suspended McGlynn from his priestly duties for a period of two weeks.

Even though George did not win the election, he made a strong showing. And in the wave of enthusiasm that swept over the reformer's followers, McGlynn held the spotlight. Newspapers ultimately found out about his suspension and aired various angles of the not-too-pleasant story. On November 19, 1886, at the close of the Fifth Synod of the archdiocese of New York, Archbishop Corrigan issued a pastoral letter. Such a letter was a normal thing. It treated of a number of topics, defended the right of private property, and quoted an encyclical of Pope Leo XIII on the subject. But it also warned against "socialistic theories." The pastoral did not name names, but people assumed that Corrigan was refering to the errors of Henry George and his single-tax advocates.[3]

Matters heated up as the winter got colder. McGlynn refused to stop his public addresses on the single tax. Corrigan suspended him a second time. On December 6 a summons came for McGlynn to go to Rome. He refused to obey the summons and maintained that there was nothing in George's teaching or in his own that conflicted with Church doctrines. Until the archbishop lifted the suspension, he would not comply with Corrigan's orders or those of the Holy See, since to do so would be to admit that his superior was correct in penalizing him. McGlynn did not go to Rome, and he offered no excuse for not going. He simply denied the right of his archbishop or other ecclesiastical superior to order him overseas on some unspecified charges connected with his exercise of the rights of an American citizen.[4]

McGlynn certainly could have made a case for himself. His fault was either participating in a political campaign, as Archbishop Corrigan seemed to say, or in advocating a questionable land theory, as Cardinal Simeoni charged. If the first, what in a man's priesthood deprived him of his right as an American citizen to advocate one candidate over another? If the second, was there any proportion between teaching such a land theory and going across the ocean to vindicate that theory? Did the great archdiocese of New York not have adequate procedures to judge such a case? Wasn't Rome a court of last resort, not an initial tribunal? And what of due process? And subsidiarity? And other aspects of a well-ordered society? Why did Rome receive so many complaints at this time from priests who had trouble with their bishops, as the eminent historian John Tracy Ellis asked in his *Life of James Cardinal Gibbons*?[5] Even if Rome did, as Ellis noted, usually give its judgment *against* the bishops, should any well-ordered society have asked its functionaries to go through such an elaborate procedure?

Had Rome summoned any priest for living in luxury? or in adultery? or for indulging in national and racial enmities—so common in those days? What, after all, had McGlynn said in concrete terms but this: that if New York decided to bridge the Hudson River from Mr. Traver's truck farm, then indeed the increased value of Mr. Traver's acres stemmed not from his own careful cultivation of the soil but from the community's collective decision? To see this did not take a degree in philosophy or a cardinalitial decision.

Furthermore, if God made the air, the water, and the land, and no one could take exclusive use of the skies and the seas, why could some men have land they didn't need and couldn't use, while others had none? Certainly there could be a more just way of allotting land for man's use.

But authority, not sociology, would decide the issue. After discussing the matter with the archdiocesan consultors, Corrigan removed McGlynn from the pastorate of St. Stephen's Church on January 14, 1887. Two days later a cablegram arrived from Cardinal Simeoni commanding McGlynn to retract publicly his land theory and to come immediately to Rome.

The widespread national attention that was attracted to the case between the time of the Henry George campaign and McGlynn's removal from his pastorate caused many others grave concern. Bishop John Moore of St. Augustine, Florida, a friend of McGlynn's, visited New York and shortly afterward wrote to the recently appointed Cardinal, James Gibbons of Baltimore. Moore believed that both sides had blundered.[6]

Gibbons did not meet with McGlynn, but he did see McGlynn's adviser, Father Richard Burtsell, and talked with Archbishop Corrigan in New York before leaving for Rome to receive the "Red Hat," the emblem of his new dignity. He advised Burtsell to urge McGlynn to go to Rome, not as to a trial, but as an opportunity to explain his views.[7]

During Gibbons's first audience with the Holy Father, Leo XIII asked him about McGlynn. The pope insisted that Rome had not prejudged the case and urged the New York priest to obey the summons. On the following evening, February 14, 1887, Gibbons had an interview with Cardinal Simeoni in much the same vein.[8] He communicated this information to Corrigan and to Burtsell.[9]

While in Rome, Gibbons heard that the Index of Prohibited Books would soon include Henry George's theories. Gibbons took this matter up with Cardinal Simeoni. He contended that George was not the originator of his theories; Herbert Spencer and John Stuart Mill had expressed similar ideas. The world would surely find it strange if the Holy See would attack a work of an American craftsman-reformer instead of condemning the writings of his European masters. Secondly, Gibbons insisted that George's theories differed from those of Communism and Socialism. He further remarked that the Americans were a pragmatic people, less concerned with theories and more concerned with practice. Henry George had said that only by legislation would his theories have a chance, and he had lost the election. Gibbons suggested that the Roman authorities leave the whole matter to the decision of the American electorate. And he concluded by saying that a condemnation would give George's writings an importance they would never otherwise enjoy.[10]

While Cardinal Gibbons was exerting himself in Rome to prevent the condemnation of Henry George's writings, the affair of Father McGlynn and Archbishop Corrigan grew progressively worse. The priest's removal from his pastorate had enraged his friends, both Catholic and non-Catholic. They held open demonstrations in his favor. Even the clergy took sides. McGlynn's public statements grew more intemperate. Many feared he would leave the Church entirely. McGlynn gave stirring speeches during the ensuing days. In March he spoke on the "Cross of a New Crusade" to an enthusiastic audience. Many New York priests were on the platform during this speech. And this irritated the Archbishop; he reprimanded and ultimately disciplined several of them. This led to further recriminations in the press on both sides.[11] In the same month McGlynn made a statement at the memorial services for the late Henry Ward Beecher. Bishops all over the country expressed their concern about the situation. Even Corrigan himself began to speak in more severe terms. He wrote to Cardinal Gibbons: "It is an ulcer that needs the knife; nothing less vigorous will be successful."[12]

McGlynn told his followers that at the time of his suspension from St. Stephen's, the Archbishop had actually offered him the care of the parish at Middleton, New York.[13] "No power on earth," he went on, "can excommunicate a child of God from God unless with the consent of that child himself. There are only two beings in all the universe who can separate me from my God, one is God himself, and the other is Edward McGlynn. God is all-wise and all-merciful, and he will not do it unless Edward McGlynn so wills it, and that I will never do! . . . This lightning is stage lightning; this thunder is stage thunder. I know enough of canonical law to know that an unjust excommunication cannot stand, and the thing has been proven many times before."[14] McGlynn frequently spoke of the demands of his conscience. He would do what his conscience told him to do, even if churchmen told him not to do so.

All the while Cardinal Gibbons in Rome was not finding his role as peacemaker an easy thing. He had many items of business pertaining to the American Church—the question of the Knights of Labor, to mention just one—besides the McGlynn affair. Then, too, he had the business of his own archdiocese to transact.

American newspapers pictured Cardinal Gibbons as a defender of McGlynn against Corrigan, and they tried to split the two men on grounds that were based on little more than hearsay.[15] And in the background was the rivalry between New York, the largest diocese in the country, and Baltimore, the oldest. And Corrigan's predecessor, not Gibbons's had been a cardinal.

On March 11, Father Burtsell, as McGlynn's canonical advocate, cabled a reply that his client would go to Rome on certain conditions. At the same time he wrote a long letter to Cardinal Gibbons in Rome, explaining fully the canonical situation from McGlynn's viewpoint. For reasons that seemed good to him, Cardinal Gibbons did not present either the cablegram or the letter to the Roman authorities, contenting himself with an oral statement of their contents. Actually, the Cardinal was not authorized to act as an intermediary between McGlynn and his Archbishop, as he himself was to state in an interview later on that year.[16]

Failing to receive any written reply from McGlynn, the pope ordered him to come to Rome within forty days under penalty of excommunication. The forty days expired without McGlynn's making any move to comply with the Roman com-

mand. On July 8, 1887, Archbishop Corrigan issued a statement
that the priest had incurred excommunication. He claimed that he
was merely following a directive and insisted that the whole
matter of excommunication had originated in Rome without any
suggestion from him.[17]

Father McGlynn came out fighting. He went forward with
speaking tours for the Anti-Poverty Society that followers of
Henry George had organized in March, even though Corrigan
had forbidden the Catholics of the archdiocese to attend its meetings. At the Brooklyn Opera House, on July 31, McGlynn delivered a scathing attack on the "ecclesiastical machine" in the
United States and in Rome. He called his talk, "The New
Know-Nothingism and the Old." He used the same subject and
the same title for an article in the *North American Review* the
following month.

McGlynn opened fire in many directions. First he attacked German immigrant Catholics for not being one hundred
percent American, for using German language in their schools,
and for trying to "Germanize the Catholic Church in the Northwest."[18] He criticized a certain Professor Boyesen and Labor
leader Terence Powderly for wanting to limit immigration. He
condemned the use of ducal titles and vesture by bishops and for
forcing "the priests to wear, in public as well as in private, a
professional badge known as the Roman collar."[19] Then he repeated his pro-public school views, and condemned the growing
Catholic hostility to public schools. Next he denounced the attempt of Italian ecclesiastical authorities to impose the burden of
supporting parochial schools on the American people while not
daring to impose a similar burden on their own people.

All these scatter-shot attacks faded before his main denunciation. The mistake that might trigger a new burst of
Know-Nothingism, he believed, was "the actual and direct interference in politics of bishops, vicar generals and priests in their
ecclesiastical capacity."[20]

McGlynn could cite many such acts of interference. He
chose to mention these: "the denunciation of one of the candidates and his party from Catholic altars; the secret prohibition to a
priest, who went not as a priest, but as a citizen, to keep his
engagement to speak at a political meeting . . . ; the abuse of the
confessional in forbidding men under penalty of refusal of

absolution to attend the meetings of one political party; and last and worst of all, the effort of an archbishop in the late election to defeat at the polls by the abuse of his ecclesiastical position the call for a constitutional convention, which, as the result proved, was demanded by an overwhelming majority of all those who voted on this question . . ."[21]

And in case anyone had any doubts about the name of that archbishop, McGlynn spoke of him as the same prelate who had, as Bishop of Newark some years before, interfered with the free electoral choices of his people in the state of New Jersey. The prelate was, of course, Archbishop Michael Corrigan. McGlynn saw Tammany Hall as the "ally of the ecclesiastical machine."[22] McGlynn concluded that the alleged dangers that the early Know-Nothings thought they saw were a hundred times more real with "the growth of an ecclesiastical power, secret and despotic in its methods."[23]

McGlynn seemed to lash out in every direction in this article; and yet in his main point, he made a clear distinction between the political action of a clergyman as a citizen (the capacity he chose for himself) and the use by a clergyman of his religious position to further a political cause (the posture Archbishop Corrigan chose to assume).

For five years excommunication deprived the people of New York of the services of one of their most talented and dedicated priests. McGlynn lived at the home of his sister and spoke regularly at the meetings of the Anti-Poverty Society.

In 1889 the Holy Office gave a revolving door answer to the teachings of Henry George: the theories deserved condemnation; but no one should make public such a ban. In 1892 Pope Leo sent Archbishop Francisco Satolli to the United States in the capacity of papal ablegate to settle the Minnesota school controversy that arose from Archbishop Ireland's attempt to institute a plan similar to the one Bishop Augustine Verot had worked out successfully in Savannah years before.

Doctor McGlynn submitted to Archbishop Satolli a statement of what he taught on the land question. Satolli asked for an expert opinion from four professors at the Catholic University of America where he resided. Professors Thomas Bouquillon, Thomas O'Gorman, Edward A. Pace, and Charles P. Grannan examined the statement in light of the recent labor encyclical, *Rerum*

Novarum, and of Church teachings in general. They found nothing in the statement against faith and morals. Satolli received McGlynn at the university on December 23, 1892, and later that evening, basing his judgment on the professors' analysis, he issued a statement to the press that freed the priest from ecclesiastical censures and restored to him the exercise of his priestly functions.

With the lifting of the ban, McGlynn went to Florida a few weeks later. He preached and gave lectures in the diocese of St. Augustine under the friendly patronage of his loyal defender, Bishop John Moore. The impression McGlynn made elated the bishop, and people received him warmly on all sides.

The following summer McGlynn made the long-delayed trip to Rome. Pope Leo XIII received him kindly, as did his Secretary of State Cardinal Rampolla. McGlynn had high praise for the establishment of a permanent Apostolic Delegation in the United States with Satolli as delegate. He also took the occasion to say that the presence in the country of the pope's representative would put a stop to the tyranny practiced by some bishops in governing their priests and people.[24]

A year and a half of uncertainty with regard to his status in the Archdiocese of New York followed his return from Rome. Finally in January 1895, Corrigan appointed him pastor of St. Mary's Church at Newburg, New York. In February 1897, he contributed an article to the *Forum,* giving a glowing account of Satolli's mission as Apostolic Delegate to the United States.[25] The article appeared two months after Satolli had become a cardinal and had returned to Rome. Both Cardinal Satolli and Cardinal Rampolla sent letters of appreciation to the author. He, in turn, sent them on to the archbishop of Baltimore, whom he presumed would be pleased to see them.[26]

In October 1897, Father McGlynn pronounced the eulogy at the funeral of his old friend Henry George. The two men had fallen out for a number of years, but they were reconciled before George's death. In the meantime, as Cardinal Gibbons had predicted, the enthusiasm for his crusade had waned. Although a few of George's followers continued their interest, the movement had ceased to occupy national attention.

Over the years, Doctor McGlynn and Archbishop Corrigan never developed a complete friendship. They did meet on several occasions and talked about Church matters. But the remarks of some of Corrigan's friends did not help. Cardinal Gibbons's intervention had roused the archbishop's ire. Gibbons's detailed explanations of his actions, his oral apologies given through Archbishop Patrick Ryan, and occasional friendly gestures seemed to do little to thaw the coldness. Historian John Tracy Ellis saw only a formal politeness that lacked entirely the suggestion of genuine forgiveness and a satisfaction of mind.[27]

Edward McGlynn, the "rebel priest," died on Sunday morning, January 7, 1900. His longstanding friend, Father Richard L. Burtsell, arrived just a few minutes later. McGlynn's funeral in Newburg proved one of the most impressive events ever seen in the Hudson River Valley. Within and without the spacious church of St. Mary's, people of all and no denominational identifications gathered to honor him. The clergy and the one Jewish rabbi of the city marched in a body to seats reserved for them. Father Burtsell gave the eulogy. He stated that as a citizen of this great American nation, Edward McGlynn had an inalienable right to think and speak of all things that were for the good of the people. It was his duty so long as he followed God's guidance. Holy Church wanted us to promote the welfare of the country. "It is therefore the duty of all," Father Burtsell concluded. "He was glad to respond to it."[28]

From Newburg, friends took Father McGlynn's body to St. Stephen Church in New York City, where his old parishioners came to pay their tribute of love and honor to the priest they devoutly believed they had lost without just cause. Archbishop Corrigan gave the final blessing in the Old Calvary Cemetery in the Bronx. In this beautiful setting, in 1918, his friends erected an heroic statue of Father Edward McGlynn, the work of sculptor Edmund T. Quinn.

CHAPTER 6

BLACK PROTÉGÉ OF A FIGHTING ARCHBISHOP

Stephen L. Theobald (1874–1932)

Stephen Theobald never had to take a stand against the local ecclesiastical establishment; but he and his archbishop had to stand together against the color line of the entire country.

Stephen Theobald could not boast that he was the first black priest in the United States. That honor belongs either to the mulatto bishop of Portland, Maine, James Augustine Healy, D.D., or to the son of Missouri slaves, Father Augustine Tolton, pastor of St. Monica's Colored Parish in Chicago in the last part of the nineteenth century.

Stephen Theobald first alerted the nation by breaking the color line in American diocesan seminaries. Both Bishop Healy and Father Tolton had studied theology in Europe, the former at the Sulpician Seminary in Paris, the latter at the Seminary of the Propaganda in Rome. The other black priests who preceded Father Theobald belonged to religious institutes.[1]

Stephen Theobald's admission to the seminary stemmed from the strong stand Archbishop John Ireland of St. Paul had taken on the racial question. When colored Catholics began to have a series of annual conventions in the early 1890s, Archbishop Ireland had given them unqualified support. America had only finished half its task, he said, with the emancipation of the blacks.

51

He called for education and the opening of all professional and industrial avenues to Negroes.

"I know no color lines," Ireland said on one occasion. "I will acknowledge none. I am not unaware that this solemn declaration of mine shall be deemed by many, upon whose opinion I set high value, as rash and untimely. Yet I fear not to make it. I am ahead of my day. But the time is not distant when Americans and Christians will wonder that there ever was race prejudice."[2]

This was not the first provocative stance of the great fighting archbishop of the Northwest. Archbishop Ireland had opposed Catholic schools—sometimes in intemperate language—in favor of an alternative that he thought would better serve the Church and the country in the long run. He had taken a position on the relationship of the Church and the State that many people in Europe and America misunderstood and misinterpreted. He was a man who lived in controversy—and may well have been at least a century "ahead of his day."

Inevitably, his remarks on the race question brought out this question: "Would you admit a colored student into your seminary?"

John Ireland thundered, "Yes!"

"Suppose a large number of students should object or embarrass this student. What then?"

"I would expel all such students," the Archbishop exploded, "for their act would prove conclusively to me that they were unworthy of the high office to which they aspire. There is no room in the Catholic Church for racial prejudice."[3]

Such was the background in the St. Paul diocese when Stephen Theobald, a native of Georgetown in British Guiana, who had just finished his law degree at Cambridge, applied for admission to the diocesan seminary in 1905. He became Archbishop Ireland's special protégé. They made an extraordinary team: the fighting archbishop, with his leonine countenance, looking ready at any moment to challenge the entire world; and the diminutive, quiet, bespectacled scholar who would gladly have lived his life in placid waters, had not America's racial pattern called for reform. And even in his reform efforts, unlike his archbishop, Stephen Theobald worked inconspicuously behind the scenes, urging and guiding laymen in the struggle. Only in two public statements was he to reveal the intensity of his convictions.

Archbishop Ireland ordained Stephen Theobald a priest on June 8, 1910, and assigned him to the cathedral staff to work on canon law cases. Soon he was made the pastor of St. Peter Claver's Church in St. Paul. He was to serve this integrated congregation for the remaining twenty-two years of his life, and he would move out from there into the wider work of race relations throughout the country.

In 1914, Father Theobald met Dr. Thomas W. Turner in Baltimore. Dr. Turner spoke of organizing a federation of colored Catholics along the lines of the National Association for the Advancement of Colored People (NAACP). Father Theobald was enthusiastic. He supported Dr. Turner and other Catholic Negro leaders who laid plans for a united effort. These leaders asked Father Theobald to represent the Catholics at the NAACP's annual convention."[4]

Dr. Turner, Father Theobald, and their friends took their first organizational steps with the "Committee Against the Extension of Race Prejudice in the Church." Father Theobald served as spiritual director of this group. It used the press and personal correspondence in a campaign against racism among Catholics. The members bombarded the Apostolic Delegate and the American hierarchy with requests for the opening of Catholic schools, and especially seminaries, to Negroes. In 1919 the group, somewhat mellowed, altered its name to "The Committee for the Advancement of Colored Catholics," and adopted a more personal approach in calling on the archbishops and bishops of the country. Finally, in 1925, the group expanded into a national organization called the Federated Colored Catholics of the United States. It was through this organization that Father Theobald did his greatest work.

Most of his effort took place out of the limelight. He encouraged and stimulated the laymen who carried the issues before the public. He did not have that "center of the stage" quality that characterized so many other reformers. He rarely gave into a beleaguered, defensive attitude; no doubt because, with Archbishop Ireland behind him, he never felt threatened. But on two occasions he spoke out forthrightly.

The publication of a "Peter Claver Prize Essay" in the Records of the American Catholic Historical Society in June 1924 seems to have provoked the first of Father Theobald's statements.

The author, Miriam T. Murphy, covered her ground in a thorough and orderly manner, but omitted some facets of Catholic activities among the Negroes, and tended to gloss over a failure to face the real moral issue.[5] Father Theobald does not mention Miss Murphy's article. But his statement appeared in December of the same year, and it bore the identical title: "Catholic Missionary Work Among the Colored People of the United States (1776–1866)." He corrected or supplemented her material, rather than present a total historical analysis in itself.[6] He obviously wrote hurriedly, without careful regard for chronology or scholarly apparatus.

Father Theobald pointed out that almost half of the blacks living in Baltimore at the outbreak of the Civil War were already free,[7] and he told of the efforts of free Negroes to provide education for themselves. He singled out Maria Becraft of Washington, who taught Negro girls for some years before entering a convent.[8] Among deficiencies in the attitudes of white Catholics, he mentioned the isolation of the Oblate Sisters after the death of their founder, Father Jacques N. Joubert, and, far more influential, Bishop John England's insistence that the letter of Pope Gregory XVI in condemnation of the slave trade, did not condemn slavery itself as it existed in the southern states.[9] Father Theobald quoted Bishop Francis Patrick Kenrick of Philadelphia as deploring the existence of slavery and regretting restrictions on the education and religious practices of the Negroes, but, at the same time, urging no action against the laws of the land.[10] In all fairness to Bishop Kenrick, Father Theobald also pointed out that Kenrick urged emancipation of slaves when an opportunity arose to send them to Liberia.[11] In general, Catholic leaders before emancipation often insisted, given the conditions of the deep South, that a Catholic slaveholder had to make sure that in freeing a black he actually improved his lot.

"Thus it is clear," Father Theobald concluded, "that the American bishops indorsed the institution of domestic slavery basing their attitude on their interpretation of the Holy Father's letter in which, as they held, a clear distinction was made between the African slave trade and domestic slavery, and this in spite of their knowledge that apart from the alleged good treatment accorded to Catholic slaves by their owners, all the horrors of the African slave trade and still more were to be found in the institution in the south . . . In view of the foregoing, what, I may ask, becomes of Archbishop Spalding's claim that the Church stood aloof from political issues leading up to the Civil War?"[12]

Finally, Father Theobald agreed that the unwillingness of the Catholic Church to find a place for the Negro preacher after the Civil War proved disastrous. "There was better prospect for promotion in the Baptist and Methodist churches and to those two churches went the would-be Negro preacher and through his influence the majority of his people."[13]

Had Father Theobald been a white man, he would probably have lived the routine life of a city pastor. Unlike Father O'Leary, who was a rebel at heart, he was a gentle, reserved man in his approach. Unlike Father William Markoe, who invited him to celebrate the main Mass at the Convention of the Federated Colored Catholics in St. Louis in 1931, Father Theobald did not like to disturb the sensibilities of his associates.

This natural reserve showed itself in his address, "Our Hopes and Aspirations," given at the St. Louis University gymnasium on the night of September 6, 1931. Yet in the former slave state of Missouri that at that time had not yet seen its last lynching, Stephen Theobald uttered some strong words: "Our chief problem is with our white friends . . . ," he stated. "We have shown our determination to besiege them in their citadel and we are going to sit out this siege until they give in. Their bulwarks are gradually crumbling, and we hope that in a short time they . . . will say we are right and of their own initiative they will yield what we ask for. It is nothing but justice, nothing but justice."[14]

Father Theobald had complete faith in the Church. "Although local tendencies may compel recognition of race prejudices, it (the Church) will not capitulate to it," he said, quoting another interracial leader.[15] Otherwise it would lose its claim to catholicity. He then launched out boldly against local segregation. "Right here in St. Louis, you will see instances in Catholic institutions in which the line is drawn, especially on education, " he said. "Of course, according to the law of the state the schools provide for the separate education of its youth. The Catholic schools are private schools under the direct control of the Church, and yet, I am informed, we are not allowed an opportunity to seek their education . . . In our hospitals controlled by religious women . . . colored Catholics are not admitted." He closed his litany of discriminations with a prediction about the university on

55

whose campus he spoke: "With the tide of things trending in the right direction now, it will not be many years when we shall be able to witness the presentation of diplomas from St. Louis University to our boys and girls."[16]

The gymnasium reverberated with applause at this point, and, a few minutes later, when Father Theobald concluded his talk.

Back in St. Paul, the devoted pastor Stephen Theobald promoted novenas to the Little Flower of Jesus, Ste. Therese of Lisieux, then enjoying a heyday of interest. Many people of other parishes joined with his own in these devotions. He served as confessor of sisters. He joined with his fellow priests in a spirit of warm camaraderie that reflected the fine ideals of Archbishop Ireland.

Just after Father Theobald celebrated his twenty-second anniversary as pastor of St. Peter Claver, appendicitis struck him in the summer of 1932. He went to the hospital on the eighth of June. Archbishop John A. Murray stayed near his bedside much of the succeeding four days until his death on July 12.

Five bishops and more than a hundred priests attended his funeral. Ushers had to turn away over a thousand mourners from the already filled church. He had built a deep spirituality among his own parishioners, black and white. He had given to Colored Catholics throughout the country encouragement and hope.

He was externally the least rebellious of all rebel priests. He had no particular adversary in his rebellion. He fought the unjust pattern of an entire nation. He helped to open doors for others to follow.

CHAPTER 7

SOUND SOCIAL LEGISLATION

John Augustine Ryan (1869–1945)

Social scientists may discuss whether the times proved right for John Augustine Ryan or whether he was right for the times. But no one doubts that his country and his Church needed an ethical spokesman who could pronounce on social and economic issues at the time he appeared on the scene.

Had he come a generation earlier, or grown up in the territory of a less progressive archbishop than John Ireland of St. Paul, he may have "sweated it out" in a dead-end canyon, frustrated and ineffective. Had the Great Depression of 1929 not brought untrammelled capitalism into disrepute, he may never have lived to see so many of the social reforms he advocated embodied in national and state laws. But he and the times came together.

The oldest of eleven children of Irish immigrants, William and Mary Luby Ryan, young John grew up on a Minnesota farm. He attended a local public school and the Christian Brothers high school in neighboring St. Paul. He entered St. Thomas Seminary in 1887 when Populist spellbinders such as Ignatius Donnelly, a fellow Minnesotan and Irish Catholic, fought to improve the lot of American farmers. Always interested in politics, John Ryan read *Rerum Novarum* in 1894, three years after its publication and called it a turning point in his life. The country boy who might have become an expert on farm problems began to look at ethical issues in industry.

After Archbishop Ireland ordained him in 1898, young Father Ryan went to The Catholic University in Washington, D.C. There he earned his licentiate in moral theology, graduating *maxima cum laude* in 1902. In pursuing his doctorate, he came under the tutelage of a Belgian ethician, Father Thomas Bouquillon, who covered a wide range of moral questions. Father William J. Kerby, a professor about the same age as Ryan, and a fellow Midwesterner, also proved a guide as he continued toward his doctorate.

Father Ryan came to see the immorality in certain monopolistic practices. He explored the question of "fair price." He saw the difference in usury in the Old Testament when the psalmist condemned it, and in modern days when the Church allowed the practice. In earlier times when consumers borrowed to get enough to survive, many lenders took advantage of the temporary misfortune of his fellowman to gain a profit. In modern times many men borrowed money to begin new enterprises, to open new markets, or to create new products. In such a situation money was a creative commodity not just a medium of exchange.

The strapping Minnesotan wrote his dissertation on the ethical and economic aspects of the living wage. It was hardly a topic the Astors or Vanderbilts discussed at length in their Newport, Rhode Island, summer mansions. But its ideas far outlived other contemporary writings. In the meantime, before receiving his doctorate in 1906, Ryan had returned to St. Paul to teach in the seminary. In 1909 he drew up a seven-point program for social reform by legislation in an article in the *Catholic World*. He called for: (1) a legal minimum wage; (2) a law establishing an eight-hour day; (3) protective legislation for women and children; (4) legislation to protect peaceful picketing and boycotting; (5) the establishment of employment bureaus and arranging for insurance to cover periods of unemployment; (6) provision against accident, illness, and old age; and (7) municipal housing.[1]

The St. Paul social reformer came to feel that his fellow Catholics spent too much time in answering Karl Marx and gave too little attention to solving the social problems that had given Marx his worldwide audience. Father Ryan had a second misgiving about his fellow Catholics. Too many Catholic clerics, he believed, took the loyalty of the Catholic workers for granted; whereas, in his experience, it seemed that Protestant leaders were more apt to be aware of the danger of losing workers for many of the same reasons that European churches, Catholic and Protestant, had lost them during the previous century.

Father Ryan joined social reform organizations, such as the National Consumers League, lectured widely, and wrote for a variety of periodicals. He contributed the article on labor organizations to the *Catholic Encyclopedia*. To a nation that still thought of unions as conspiracies in restraint of trade, and whose courts prosecuted unions more than trusts under the Sherman Anti-Trust Act of 1890, Ryan faced countless grim visages facading closed minds in and out of the Church, including members of his own clerical ranks. But he had ideals and a message to bring before the public. He debated Morris Hillquit, the socialist writer, on reform issues. Ryan's position, published under the title *Socialism: Promise or Menace?* in 1914, became a minor classic.

Father Ryan's earlier proposals had reflected the type of legislation the reform government of England was promoting at the time. His next group of proposals were derived from the American experience. They reflected the views of either the Populists of the 1890s, or the progressive Republicans in the early decades of the century, or of those advocated by President Woodrow Wilson during his first term (1912–1916). Father Ryan called for public ownership of mines, forests, and public utilities; control of monopolies by breaking them up or by fixing prices; progressive income and inheritance taxes; prohibition of speculation on the stock and commodity exchanges; and taxation of the future increase in land values—a recommendation that showed his respect for the theories of Henry George. But unlike Edward McGlynn, he underwent no penalties for approving of Henry George's theories.

When Ryan joined the faculty of Catholic University during World War I, he started out in political science. Later he moved to moral theology. In 1916 he analyzed ethical obligations of all parties in a modern industrial society in his most substantial work, *Distributive Justice*. In a day when management, labor, and stockholders upheld their own claims with little concern for their interrelationships, Ryan looked at the issues with a balanced and all-encompassing eye.

With World War I in progress and businessmen anxious to keep the workers working, profits profiting, and stocks stockpiling, Father Ryan founded the *Catholic Charities Review* and drew up the "Bishops' Program of Social Reconstruction." It was well timed. When the Armistice came, business and government began to move against the laboring man, cutting back on the limited gains he had won during the war. The courts were to prosecute unions as illegal trusts during the early 1920s even though the Clayton Anti-Trust Act of 1914 had expressly excluded them.

The program that the Catholic University professor drew up, which the hierarchy led by Bishop Peter Muldoon of Rockford, Illinois, issued in its own name, seems startling only when one considers the climate of the times. The program called for legal protection of labor organizations, minimum wage legislation, participation of the worker in management and ownership, public housing, unemployment, health and old age insurance, restrictions on woman and child labor, control of excessive profits and incomes through regulation of rates and progressive taxes on inheritance and income, effective control of monopolies, the establishment of cooperative stores, and the continuation of the War Labor Board that had been set up to promote better relations between workers and management during the war.

Such a program presidential candidates Socialist Eugene Debs in 1920, Progressive Republican Senator Robert La Follette in 1924, and Democrat Governor Alfred E. Smith in 1928 might have supported had they won; but not the leaders Americans chose as their presidents in the 1920s, the Republicans Warren Harding, Calvin Coolidge, and Herbert Hoover. A committee of the State Senate of New York, which was investigating seditious activities, condemned the program. The Lusk Committee (named for Senator Clayton R. Lusk, the chairman) stated that the socialist tendency of the group of Catholics, under "the leadership of the Rev. Dr. Ryan," showed itself clearly in the areas of cooperation and copartnership.[2]

When the New York legislature expelled five Socialist assemblymen, Ryan congratulated Morris Hillquit, their attorney, and supported these duly elected men. Ryan's position seemed to have few allies in those post-war witch-hunting days. But time would prove Ryan right.

In 1919 Ryan became Dean of the School of Theology at The Catholic University, and published *The Church and Socialism*. The next year he coedited with Joseph Husslein, S.J., a collection of social documents, entitled *The Church and Labor*. Even more important, he became director of the Social Action Department of the National Catholic Welfare Council (later Conference), a post he would hold until his death.

Accustomed to look on the social reforms that Father Ryan sought as taken-for-granted aspects of American life, modern readers can hardly appreciate the battle he and his allies had in working toward them during the 1920s. One of the Western archbishops was to say openly years later: One never knows what those 'pinkos' at the NCWC are going to say next."[3] That archbishop was aiming his arrows at Ryan, not at the advocates of liturgical reform.

From his office at the NCWC, the formidable looking but approachable Minnesotan continued to teach, write, lecture, and organize. He flooded Catholic magazines with the ideas of *Rerum Novarum* and the "Bishops' Program." He helped organize the Catholic Association for International Peace in a world that was dead set at resuming the fighting left off at the Armistice.

Father Ryan joined interfaith groups in pursuit of social justice, serving often on governing boards. He was never quite able to make the American Civil Liberties Union recognize that freedom of religion was a liberty worth supporting. Nor could he convince those self-proclaimed liberals that most American Catholics belonged to "the party of social concern," the Democrats, and that the Catholic Church encouraged a positive and progressive social program. The "liberals" ignored *Quadragesimo Anno* of 1931 as they had disregarded *Rerum Novarum* of 40 years before and ignored the "Bishops' Program" of 1919. Ryan's biographer, Francis J. Broderick, S.J., fittingly described Ryan's association with such fellow reformers in these words: "Father John A. Ryan ran with his liberal friends without ever joining them."[4]

Though his work with the NCWC gradually took him away from on-campus activities of the university, his views sometimes brought strong opposition from would-be wealthy benefactors. One Catholic industrialist who gave twenty million to Catholic causes gave nothing to The Catholic University. But the church authorities who governed the university continued to support Ryan. And he clung tenaciously to his academic position. With one foot on The Catholic University campus and the other in the offices of the NCWC, he always spoke and wrote from a position of strength. Furthermore, his main social views reflected the thought of Leo XIII's *Rerum Novarum* and, later on, of Pius XI's *Quadragesimo Anno*.

The Great Depression in October 1929 brought about a change in the public mind toward social reform. Though an anti-spender, President Herbert Hoover launched a program of public works totaling two and a quarter billion dollars. The most imposing of these was the beginning of the dam on the Colorado River on the border of Arizona and Nevada. Voted by Congress in the days of Coolidge, it began under Hoover in 1930 and eventually came to bear his name.

Plagued at first by a Congress more conservative even than he was, Hoover was finally able to get legislative advances in 1932: (1) the establishment of the Reconstruction Finance Corporation that made loans to businesses; (2) the Norris-LaGuardia Anti-Injunction Act that outlawed "yellow-dog" contracts, so-called because they included a pledge not to join a union, and expressly forbade the federal courts to issue injunctions against strikes, boycotts, and peaceful picketing. But the president adhered to an economic outlook that kept him from directly aiding the starving poor, the foreclosed farmers, or the unemployed urban workers. Ryan could not support him.

While the prevailing economic thought of the times saw overproduction as the problem, Father Ryan believed it was underconsumption. Don't restrict the scope of the producer, he urged. Increase the buying power of the consumer. With the election coming up in 1932, Ryan turned from criticizing Hoover to looking at the nominees. Socialist Norman Thomas usually spoke in the most straightforward, consistent, and hopeful manner. But the country was not yet ready for a socialist president. Franklin D. Roosevelt spent a lot of time during his early campaign days criticizing Hoover's excessive spending. Ryan gave his personal support to Newton D. Baker, Secretary of War during Wilson's administration.

When Roosevelt took the oath of office in March 1932, his inaugural address encouraged Ryan, now a monsignor. Over the next few months, Ryan grew close to many of the New Deal personnel in Washington, most of whom he had not previously known. Eventually, he became an enthusiastic New Dealer. The new domestic prelate served as a member of the Industrial Appeals Board of the National Recovery Administration, FDR's initial device to get the economy moving.

Father Ryan looked on the National Labor Relations Act, the famous Wagner Act of 1935, as the greatest piece of labor legislation ever enacted in the United States. It created a powerful new National Labor Relations Board and reasserted the right of labor to organize and bargain collectively.

The Fair Labor Standards Act of 1938 brought further improvements, including minimum wage and maximum hour levels, and restrictions on hiring children. Previously such welfare legislation had run afoul of the Supreme Court. This law sailed through without trouble and was subsequently upheld by the Court. Ryan felt that the Fair Labor Standards Act culminated his life's work.

Even though he based his social theories solidly on the papal social encyclicals, Ryan faced much opposition both from the industrialists of whatever religion who cared little for the welfare of the laboring man and from his fellow Catholics who did not share his enthusiasm for New Deal reform programs. When he and the radio orator Father Charles Coughlin debated public views, Ryan received over eleven hundred abusive letters. An Eastern Catholic paper suggested both "political priests" could well spend some time with the Carthusians in perpetual silence.

During the 1940 election, Ryan reluctantly refrained from giving public support to President Roosevelt, adhering to the non-partisan position of the NCWC. He could rejoice, however, in the publication of "The Church and Social Order," the bishops' statement that endorsed almost every social reform he had supported for two decades.

In 1941 Harper and Brothers published Ryan's autobiography that he entitled *Social Doctrine in Action*. By that time, many other Catholics, priests and laymen, took a direct part in industrial reform: labor school directors, union leaders, editors, businessmen, college professors, parish priests, workers, teachers, nuns, congressmen, senators, state governors, and cabinet members.

Monsignor Ryan could take heart that the campaigns he had begun almost single-handedly thirty years before, now numbered many supporters. He had succeeded in bringing Catholics abreast of progressive thought on social and economic questions. By his last days, a month after the end of World War II, he could look back with satisfaction to a rare position among Catholic social reforming clergymen. Long before his death, he could see the accomplishment of most of his life goals.

CHAPTER 8

A SEGREGATED CITY

William Markoe (1892–1970)

William Markoe never bragged that his ancestors were
wealthy planters in the French West Indies. Instead, as a young
man in his native Minnesota, he began to regret his ancestral
heritage and tried to make reparation for what he thought was the
ill-gotten gain of his ancestors who employed black slaves on
their three plantations.

At the age of twenty-one, William Markoe gave up all his
own possessions and the possibility of future wealth by taking a
vow of poverty in the Society of Jesus at the Jesuit novitiate at
Florissant, Missouri, and he made a special promise to commit
his life to improving the lot of the black people. His brother, John
Markoe, captain of the famed West Point football team of 1912
that included future World War II heroes Dwight "Ike" Eisenhower, Carl "Towey" Spaatz, and Omar Bradley, followed
William's example by also becoming a Jesuit. So did his friend
Augustine Bork, who—though less conspicuous—was no less a
man of consummate compassion.

William Markoe and his associates did not wait until they
had finished their seminary course to start their work. During the
summers, they began to spend their free days visiting poor black
people scattered over the Missouri river bottoms and in segregated neighborhood settlements. They helped Protestants and Catholics alike, and they found many blacks religiously uncommitted.

These they taught catechism, and they prepared about thirty people for baptism.

Markoe studied at Gonzaga University in Spokane, Washington, and then taught at St. Francis Mission among the Brule Sioux in South Dakota for several years—an integral part of his Jesuit training. He confessed later in life that he felt like a foreigner among the Sioux. He was never to feel that way among black people.[1]

In 1923 he began divinity studies at St. Louis University, an urban university, segregated like all Missouri schools at that time, but adjacent to a black neighborhood that had grown extensively with the influx of wartime workers from the South. "Approximately half of these people were affiliated with no church and had never been baptized," Markoe wrote. "These people never knew that they could be Catholics. They thought that the Catholic Church was a white man's church. Here they were, living in a great, metropolitan, largely Catholic community, many of them for generations, and they did not even know that they could be Catholics, much less had they been invited to become such." Markoe asked his Jesuit confreres, "Why did we deliberately pursue the Indian to save his soul, and at the same time . . . bypass the thousands of thousands of religiously inclined Negroes who were at our doorstep?"[2]

Markoe joined a team of catechists led by his colleague Augustine Bork at St. Elizabeth's, a Jesuit-staffed parish eight blocks east of the university. The group soon included a dozen other Jesuit scholastics, a group of black public school teachers, and fifty adult men and women, white and black, working at four different centers.[3] Markoe wrote a life of St. Peter Claver, apostle of the slaves in the Caribbean, entitled *The Slave of the Negroes*, and submitted regular articles on race questions to *America*, a magazine published by his fellow Jesuits in New York.

In one of seventeen articles, "The Importance of Negro Leadership," Markoe described the change in black leadership from the days of Booker T. Washington to the contemporary approach of Dr. W. E. DuBois. He contrasted the number of blacks graduating from non-white Catholic colleges in the North and the few from Catholic schools. He suggested summer programs for teachers as a way to bring blacks to Catholic schools.[4]

In "A Great Migration," Markoe recounted the great

exodus from the middle South to Kansas in 1879, the move to Arkansas and Texas in 1889, and the northern migration of 400,000 black people to the cities, principally to St. Louis, Detroit, Chicago, Pittsburgh, and New York during World War I. This flight across the Mason-Dixon line would continue with over a half million fleeing to the North shortly after.

Markoe moved from an historical analysis to a confrontation with the American Church in his next article, "The Negro and Catholicism." "The Negro cannot be won to Catholicism," Markoe claimed, "except our apostolate to him be grounded on the universal principle of justice enunciated by Christ." He quoted a Negro journal that had asked if the new pope, Pius XI, would continue "to allow the American hierarchy, despite some of its noble souls, to refuse to train and ordain Negro priests."[5] Negroes where Markoe had worked and lived admired the Church, but they awaited a sign that they were welcomed.

Except for one article, "The Negro Leader and the Church," by John J. Albert, S.S.J.,[6] Markoe was the only one writing in the magazine *America* who discussed the issues facing the Church and the Negro during the early 1920s.

Later on, in the days after Vatican II, Jesuit scholastics began all kinds of projects, and Father Pedro Arrupe, the Jesuit General, gave his warm-hearted approval. But back in the early 1920s, Missouri Province Jesuit scholastics lived a monastic routine and rarely were able to engage in apostolic ventures. In spite of this, William Markoe, whose main task should have been to study theology in preparation for the priesthood, planned to open a school for Negro children in St. Nicholas Parish. He prevailed upon the Mother Superior of the Sisters of the Blessed Sacrament to send two nuns to teach in a warehouse that had once been a school. It did not have a chair, a desk, a pencil, a piece of chalk, or a blackboard. Markoe's personal account of the opening of the school pictures him as high-handed in dealing with the nuns. But the nuns had zeal and patience and teaching skills. The number of pupils rose to five hundred within a few weeks.

Sister Praxedes Wachter of the Sisters of the Blessed Sacrament, one of the first two nuns who taught at St. Nicholas School, also recalled the beginning of the school in the warehouse near St. Nicholas Parish. Her account did not reflect any outrage at Markoe's manner. She seems to have taken in stride the hard work required to bring the former school, then a warehouse, back to its original purpose. Since she had to walk eighteen blocks to school in the morning and back again in the evening, and could ride the streetcar only when it rained, other things might have seemed less painful to her. She spoke of nine or ten young Jesuits, not just the two Markoes and Augustine Bork, as helping out. Twice she mentioned: "We made lots of converts in those days. . . . "[7]

St. Louis, the center of most of William Markoe's work, was founded by Pierre Laclède in 1764. Some of the settlers brought slaves with them from the Illinois Country where they had lived. By 1800, thirty-three percent of the residents of St. Louis were blacks, and all of them were Catholics. After the Louisiana Purchase, families from the northern tier of slave states settled in outstate Missouri. Most of them were slaveholders or men who approved of slavery. They joined with some of the old-time established French families to organize Missouri as a slave territory. The Missouri Compromise allowed Missouri to enter the Union as a slave state in 1821. During the 1840s hostile legislatures outlawed the education of Missouri blacks—even freemen. The severe Anglo-American slave code gradually prevailed over the more relaxed French customs. By 1860, however, half of the Negroes in the city of St. Louis were free. Those whose parents had been slaves of the French were Catholic. But few others professed the faith.

After the Civil War, Archbishop Peter Richard Kenrick, who won recognition as the father of the immigrant, looked upon Negroes as another ethnic minority who would do better religiously if they had their own church.(He overlooked the fact that they could not have their own black pastor.) As temporary places of identification, such national parishes served a purpose. Poles or Italians or Croats could eventually move into the mainstream of Catholic life. But this was not true for the black Catholics. Furthermore, the large Catholic white population of the city had little positive influence on the black parish during its first forty years of existence. But St. Elizabeth's Church for Blacks, under the direction of Jesuit Father Ignatius Panken, had no short life. It remained a permanent feature of the Catholic community in St. Louis.

The black Oblate Sisters, who worked in the downtown

black area, could achieve only limited results. And the Sisters of
the Blessed Sacrament, who opened a school for 125 children
near St. Elizabeth's Church during World War I, hardly did any
better.

In 1916, St. Louis became the first city to vote in a
neighborhood segregation law, but Judge D. P. Dyer of St. Louis
issued a temporary injunction. This restrained the city from en-
forcing the segregation ordinance until November 5, 1917, when
the Supreme Court declared a similar law in Louisville unconsti-
tutional. The St. Louis law did not go into effect, but neighborhood covenants did what the law could not do. Race relations
moved backward.[8]

A few years later, the Apostolic Delegate to the United
States, Archbishop Fumasoni-Biondi, asked Archbishop John
Glennon what the St. Louis Archdiocese was doing for its col-
ored members. In Glennon's long report of all the things the
Archdiocese had done—relatively little in contrast to the vast
activity among whites—two currents stood out clearly.

First, the Archbishop believed that the blacks expected
and demanded equal rights in the churches and wished to eliminate the color line altogether. "Unfortunately," Archbishop
Glennon wrote, "this is impractical for the present at least in a
city such as St. Louis which is by sentiment and tradition a
southern city, and where consequently putting in operation the
demands of the colored Catholics would lead to much disturbance."[9] Second, Glennon insisted that the colored people
thought only of their rights and forgot their obligations to support
the church and the schools that had been sustained by members of
the white race.[10]

Glennon would live by this viewpoint until his death almost twenty years later. By that time Markoe had gone to other
parts of the Missouri Jesuit Province. In no speech, pastoral letter,
or other communication was Glennon to point out to white Catholics what Christ-like living would require of them on the race issue.
No Catholic high school or college in the area accepted blacks.
Neither did the Catholic hospitals. Even black nuns could not go to
the dental clinic at St. Louis University. Moreover, church authorities made no concerted effort to change this unchristian attitude
among whites of the city. As blacks moved steadily westward in
St. Louis, the few remaining white families refused to admit them

into one parish after another. Pastors looked upon the changing racial patterns as disastrous. They did not attempt to create interracial parishes. They acted as if the blacks were not there—and if the black people did come to the church, the pastors told them to go to St. Elizabeth's.

Thus both civil and ecclesiastical societies combined to keep the blacks "in their place" by the time William Markoe approached his ordination in 1926. And the opinion of the average St. Louisan reflected the civil and ecclesiastical establishments. There was no Negro priest; there was no black city official. That there might be such someday, no one even considered. Even among young people there was no difference of attitude.

Adults did not mix socially with blacks. They did not allow their children to do so either. The blacks held the low-paying positions in the city. Few whites ever had occasion to meet a well-educated Negro—and probably few thought there were any. Blacks did manual labor, hod-carrying, housecleaning, and few whites thought that these things should be otherwise.

The attitude of the average St. Louis white—Protestant, Jew, or Catholic—was not so much a positive rejection of the black person, but a total failure to see him or her as an individual with hopes, fears, talents, ambitions, aspirations, failures, successes—the whole gamut of human experience. No white even thought that a black parent might feel or worry—exactly as he did—about a son or daughter.

This was one facet of the "Spirit of St. Louis" at the time William Markoe faced a great challenge in his life: whether or not to accept the directorship of something he ideologically detested: a "Jim Crow" parish. That was truly what St. Elizabeth's was—even though no such thing should have existed. He liked to recall in later years the constant complaint of Father Vincent Dever of St. Ignatius Parish in Philadelphia, also a "Jim Crow" parish. Father Dever, Markoe related, regularly wrote to Cardinal Dougherty that he was doing a wrong thing well; and the more perfectly he did it, "the more wrong it became."[11]

Eventually, Markoe decided to accept the pastorate. "I justified my doing so from the beginning by resolving to make the parish and the city of St. Louis a national base of operations for the promotion of interracial justice and charity throughout the United States."[12] Except for a short period when he did organizational work among Negroes in various cities, he was to hold this position until 1941. All this time he was engaged in a self-denying apostolate: he was working to make his own position obsolete.

Almost from his arrival, the strong, square-built, fine-looking William Markoe put new energy into the life of St. Elizabeth's parish. He organized convert classes and vitalized the sodalities and other Catholic action groups. Besides working with his own parishioners, he preached in many other churches of the city on behalf of the Negro Apostolate.[13] On his visits to white Catholic parishes, Father Markoe often asked Ellsworth Evans, a devout Catholic and principal of one of the public elementary schools in the city, to go with him and to talk to the assembled people. Markoe presumed quite rightly that the vast majority of the audience had never before talked to an educated black person.

William Markoe liked to shock people. When many blacks moved into once all-white areas farther west, he bought property for a church and school within the parish boundaries of the most noted racist pastor. When two of Markoe's parishioners died, he became legal guardian of their daughters. Both became nuns. When he visited another city, he would call on anyone who bore the name Markoe and try to establish a relationship. Quite often these other Markoes would turn out to be blacks who had worked on the ancestral plantation. To their surprise, the priest accepted them as cousins. He enjoyed, on the occasions when he found willing companions, to take a light-skinned Negro man of his parish to dinner at a prestigious St. Louis dining room, such as the one at the Coronado Hotel, to break the "color line" without the knowledge of the management. On one such occasion, at a restaurant with a plantation motif, the waitresses were blacks who had attended the same high school as the young man. They quietly enjoyed "Father Markoe's stunt." He criticized other priests in the apostolate for not thinking as a black—as he did. Yet, in reality, many of his parishioners thought then, and still think of him, as "the Great White Father."

William Markoe would have been considered a handsome man had he not looked plain alongside his brother John, one of the most handsome men of his generation. A formidable man who did not lose his cool easily, William Markoe had to meet opposition from so many quarters and hear over and over again the same complaints, that a little temper showed up on occasion. Quite understandably, he came to see himself and his few associates as the only ones who cared. Thus he could identify all good with his own aims and purposes; and over the years he came to have less sympathy with other points of view—no matter how justifiable they might be in context. Furthermore, he was often highly critical of men the Jesuit Provincial sent to help him, blaming their difficulties on their wrong attitudes toward blacks, when often the issue might have been something quite different.

In contrasting his approach to the question of interracial justice with a nationally known colleague, Markoe stated: "He was what I called a 'safety first' man; I was rather rash and reckless. He was ultra prudent. I considered prudence as an alibi for neglect, not always a virtue, but sometimes a sin. He seemed always to enjoy the confidence of his superiors. I seemed always to make my superiors somewhat nervous and doubtful."[14]

Markoe seemed to like it that way. He differed strongly with black leader Dr. Thomas Turner, who worked for a blacks-only national organization. Markoe felt that black Catholics needed white support at that time. He underestimated Turner.

Two young ladies of the parish, Barbara Hudlin and Virginia Givens, both destined to become Sisters of Providence, directed St. Elizabeth's first musical comedy. Produced at a midtown theatre, the St. Elizabeth's musical drew large and—without precedent—integrated crowds. With the genial assistance of Father Daniel A. Lord, the St. Elizabeth young people made their musicals annual affairs with wide support from the white Catholic community.

Since a parish magazine was an ordinary part of St. Louis parochial activity at the time, Markoe began the *St. Elizabeth's Chronicle* in 1928.[15] The first issue carried stories, poems, sermonettes, and features on prominent Negroes in history.

In September 1929, William Markoe attended the national convention of the Federated Colored Catholics of the United States in Baltimore. At this meeting, the St. Elizabeth's parish *Chronicle* became the official organ of the Federation. Jesuit John La Farge, eventually to become a national leader in the interracial apostolate and editor of *America* magazine, contributed to this opening number.[16] Markoe remained editor and continued to publish the magazine in St. Louis.[17] During 1930 the

Chronicle reported 225 adult baptisms in the parish, with classes of from two to three hundred people at six catechetical centers.[18] The following year Markoe became a member of the Board of Directors of the St. Louis Urban League. Besides serving as pastor of St. Elizabeth's, promoting the welfare of blacks throughout the city, and fostering the cause of Catholicism among black people generally, he visited many cities across the country to confer with Negro Catholic leaders.

The people of St. Elizabeth's parish planned to host the seventh annual convention of the Federated Colored Catholics of the United States on September 5, 6, and 7, 1931. Markoe gave a welcoming address in the St. Louis University gymnasium where the conference held its meetings. Nearly a thousand black Catholics came from almost every state in the Union. More than forty priests who were engaged in the black apostolate attended the convention, and a black priest celebrated Mass at the College Church before an overflow crowd. Archbishop Glennon gave a short message of greeting.

It was at the evening session on September 6, after a brief welcome from President Robert S. Johnston, S.J., of St. Louis University, that Father Stephen L. Theobald, a St. Paul pastor, attacked the color line in St. Louis Catholic institutions.[19]

As an aftermath of the meeting, St. Louis University continued to show its interest in improving interracial relations by inviting the Federated Colored Catholics to present an interracial hour once a week over its radio station WEW on Sunday afternoons. At the same time, Markoe organized two significant groups: a discussion club of blacks and whites in the professions, and a fund-raising group called White Friends of Colored Catholics.

In 1932 the Federation of Colored Catholics widened its scope and membership to become the National Catholic Federation for the Promotion of Better Race Relations. In November 1932, the *Chronicle,* the official organ of the Federation, became the *Interracial Review.*[20] Early in the following year, Markoe published an article by Roy Wilkins, a young Negro destined for a long career of leadership in the interracial field.[21]

In 1933, Markoe became chairman of the Industrial Committee of the St. Louis Urban League, and in this capacity, at the request of the mayor of St. Louis, he successfully helped to arbitrate several strikes involving blacks. During these years Markoe spent much of his time as editor of the *Interracial Review* and organizer for the Interracial Federation. Finally the Catholic Interracial Council in New York, under the spiritual direction of Father John La Farge, took over full management of the *Interracial Review*. Markoe edited his last issue in September 1934.[22] A new and enlarged editorial board selected George Hunton as editor. In his autobiography, *The Manner Is Ordinary*, La Farge credited Markoe with the founding of the *Interracial Review*,[23] though later writers on La Farge's career ignored Markoe's contribution.

Markoe returned to fulltime work as pastor of St. Elizabeth's. When Father Daniel Lord began the Summer Schools of Catholic Action (SSCA) at Webster and Fontbonne Colleges, St. Elizabeth's Parish immediately sent delegates to these meetings, integrated as they were from the outset. Further, when Father Lord began musical revues in 1938 that became annual events of St. Louis cultural life, St. Elizabeth's always put on one of the feature acts of the show.

By this time nearly one hundred thousand black people lived in St. Louis, about ten percent of the entire population. Thus St. Louis had the twelfth largest black population of any city in the nation. The white population was close to fifty percent Catholic, but the black Catholics counted less than six thousand. "The general increase and rapid individual growth of Catholic institutions has been remarkable indeed," Sociologist John T. White wrote, "but apparently there has been little thought of the Negro. Neither does he possess a Catholic college of his own or a suitable high school, nor is he permitted to attend those operated for white students."[24]

In spite of the large number of seminaries, motherhouses, convents, and schools of the city in 1934, only a few were engaged in the inner-city Negro apostolate. White found only these members of religious congregations—the Oblate Sisters of Providence, the Sisters of the Blessed Sacrament, the Sisters of St. Mary, the Sisters of Notre Dame, the Helpers of the Holy Souls, five Jesuit priests, and a priest of the Society of the Divine Word—working in the interest of the six thousand black Catholics and the ninety thousand blacks of other Christian faiths.[25]

The Sisters of St. Mary of the Third Order of St. Francis,

who had been in hospital work in St. Louis since the 1870s, took a dramatic step forward in 1934. They opened the former all-white hospital, St. Mary's Infirmary, south of the Union Station in St. Louis, as the first Catholic Negro Hospital of the area.

Then too, during the late thirties groups of Negro laymen occasionally gathered for retreats at the St. Elizabeth's parish hall or in the new school. In 1940, Mr. Charles F. Vatterott, Jr., a member of the Laymen's Retreat League, the father of a large family and an innovator in the real estate business, built an eighteen-room retreat house for the use of black Catholics in a St. Louis suburb, South Kinloch Park, where Father Otto Moorman, S.J., had organized a Negro parish during the Depression.

A third influential institution, the St. Joseph Catholic High School for Negroes, opened in 1937 under the direction of Sister Anna Joseph, C.S.J., and later of Sister Ann Adelaide, C.S.J. A seminarian, Patrick Molloy, coached and counselled the boys in his spare time and began a career that was ultimately to put him, in the late 1940s and early 1950s, in relatively the same position of priestly interracial leadership occupied by William Markoe in the previous decades. These last institutions did not, of course, stem directly from Father Markoe's work; but indirectly they were part of a wide sweep of activity that he promoted.

By 1941 the area of St. Elizabeth's was totally industrial. Markoe asked the Archbishop to turn over St. Ann's, where the Negro Catholic High School was then situated, to the Negro apostolate. A good proportion of his people had recently moved into this changing neighborhood, about sixteen blocks west and eight blocks north of St. Elizabeth's. The Archbishop had another plan. About eight blocks south and five blocks west of St. Elizabeth's stood St. Malachy's, a "white" parish in a neighborhood that had been totally flooded recently with poor black immigrants from the rural South. It had been a prominent Irish parish in the late nineteenth and early twentieth centuries, but had a reputation in more recent years as the place where a parishioner had said that "they should turn the church into a pickle factory rather than give it to the Negroes."

The pickles lost. The old pastor introduced Father Markoe to his parishioners as the new pastor of St. Malachy's one Sunday in 1941. But Markoe had suspected something was amiss. He had discussed his situation with the Jesuit Provincial a short time before. The Provincial assured him that he had everything under control. He did. On the very afternoon Markoe became pastor of St. Malachy's, the Father Provincial, not liking Markoe's approach, reassigned him as Assistant Pastor in Mankato, Minnesota.[26] In later years Markoe felt a certain distinction in having the shortest pastorate in Church history. After one year in his native Minnesota and a provocative sermon on interracial justice, Father Markoe packed his bags again. The pastor thought the sermon was too strong. It probably was. Markoe went to an inner-city Denver parish where Spanish-Americans, Negroes, Indians, and Japanese driven from the West Coast because of wartime feeling, all endured the discrimination of a white Anglo-Saxon majority of citizens. Markoe promoted credit unions, worked with housing problems, co-chaired the Committee on Racial Equality, and became a member of the Board of Directors of the Urban League. But Denver and its conservative ecclesiastical establishment could not quite stomach William Markoe. He moved again; this time to Milwaukee, Wisconsin, where he taught religion at Marquette University for his remaining years.

In the meantime, St. Louis University, under the direction of his fellow Jesuits, had finally opened its doors to blacks—the first university in a former slave state to do so. His brother John had had a hand in this, as well as other men, especially Claude Heithaus, S.J., the Jesuit General Assistant, Zacheus P. Maher, and George H. Donne, S.J.

Markoe lived to see Archbishop Joseph E. Ritter, successor to Cardinal Glennon, vindicate all Markoe had stood for by integrating schools and churches throughout the city in 1948. Markoe made annual trips to St. Louis, where he had spent most of his creative years. On these occasions the Catholics who had worked with him in the crucial days met together to recall old times. It would be nice to be able to say that on one of these occasions St. Louis—city, archdiocese, or university—gave a fitting testimonial to his years of self-sacrificing service. But no one saw fit to do this. His friends gathered for the last time in 1970 to attend a memorial mass in his honor at Visitation Convent in suburban St. Louis, where his two nun sisters resided.

William Markoe had lived to see many of the things he fought for come to a successful conclusion. Interracial justice became a popular cause. But some old-timers still blamed him because a new archbishop had come in and inculcated ideas they had never liked when they first heard them from Markoe's lips a quarter of a century before. William Markoe would leave them to God. He had fought the battles when fighters were few and the cause was unpopular. And he had made reparation for all those Markoes who used slave labor on their Caribbean plantations.

Some years after he died, the St. Louis Archdiocese encouraged a study by interview of the religious origins of black Catholics. As expected, the old-line Catholics attributed much of their spiritual growth to William Markoe. To the younger generation of blacks, he was a revered pastor their parents talked about with admiration.[27]

CHAPTER 9

SOCIAL JUSTICE IN THE SOUTH

Louis Twomey (1905–1969)

Tampa-born Louis Twomey did not follow Christ's command to love one's enemy. He never granted that he had an enemy. And as to the further charge: "To do good to those who hate you," Louis Twomey had a simplified response: He did good to everyone he possibly could. If people hated his ideas on social justice, or what they thought to be an overdrawn or one-sided statement of them, he was only baffled that they did not see what was so obvious to him. People called him a "Communist and a traitor, " but he did not flail back at them or lose his optimism. He was a fighter, but he fought evil ideas, not men.

Unlike Father Cummings, Louis Twomey never went to jail for disobeying laws of the state, but he did work to have legislators in his region change the laws he did not like. Unlike Cornelius O'Leary, he never reacted testily, but he did testify throughout his life on behalf of sound labor legislation. Unlike Edward McGlynn, he never campaigned for favorite candidates, but he did everything he could to promote the good programs of these men. Unlike Stephen Theobald, he was not a black; but because he so identified his lifework with the cause of the disadvantaged, blacks throughout the nation singled him out as an extraordinary friend.

Twomey did not work exclusively in an inner-city parish as William Markoe did, but through his association with the

Institutes of Industrial Relations and Human Relations at Loyola University in New Orleans, he worked ceaselessly in the cause of blacks and workingmen, white and black.

He never questioned America's capacity and willingness to solve its own problems, and he lived to see America make tremendous advances in social justice. When he first began to work in the interests of organized labor, many Southern communities still looked upon unions as conspiracies in restraint of trade. His adult years stretched from the time the Southern delegates on President Truman's Commission on Higher Education submitted a minority report calling for continued segregation in colleges and universities to the day when qualified students entered such ancient southern citadels as the Universities of Mississippi and Alabama, regardless of their race, creed, or color.

Louis Twomey was interested in so many aspects of the quest for social justice that he could always see progress somewhere—either in the credit union movement, or in labor organizations, or having to do with race issues, or with industrial relations. Perhaps it was this battlefront concept, as opposed to the concept of other social reformers who concentrated their attention on one point of attack, that made Louis Twomey so much more sanguine about America's possibilities.

Twomey's personal joys stemmed from social advances. A professional ball player with the Washington Senators after his years at Georgetown University, he thrilled when Jackie Robinson began to line doubles against the wall at Ebbets Field. The Warren Decision proved a landmark in his life—in a way quite different from what it was in the lives of many other leading Southerners. He welcomed Pope John's *Mater et Magistra* as personal papal approval of all that he had ever stood for.

Louis Twomey received his early education at the Academy of the Holy Name in Tampa and at the local Jesuit High School. He distinguished himself in elocution by winning medals in his junior and senior years. He went to Georgetown University in Washington, D.C., where he continued to excel in public speaking and in baseball. In one game he beat Yale with an inside-the-park home run. He caught in the Washington Senators' bull pen during the summer, and in the fall of 1928 he joined the Jesuit Order at St. Charles College, Grand Coteau, Louisiana. After his course at St. Charles, he took a master's degree in

English at St. Louis University, and taught for three years at Spring Hill College in Mobile, Alabama. At St. Mary's Jesuit School of Divinity in Kansas, he studied theology in preparation for his ordination as a priest in June 1939. He then served for four years as principal of Jesuit High in Tampa, where he had been a student.

By this time he had come to the realization that something was wrong with the racial pattern in the area where he lived. Years later, in a nationally aired radio broadcast, he was to describe his early years: "I was raised in a rigidly segregated community. I accepted such an environment without question. It never occurred to me that the compulsory separation of Negro from white in every phase of human relationships was anything more than a normal arrangement . . . .

"Uncritically, I conformed to the thought and action habits of white supremacy. I did so out of loyalty, as I then believed, to what we in the South call our sacred traditions. My youthful conviction that the white race was the superior race was never challenged. And so, throughout the entire period of my formal schooling, my attitudes toward race were determined by the laws and customs of the Southern city in which I was born and raised.

"But there came a day when for the first time I began to see the basic contradiction between my belief in the equality of all men and my behavior toward the Negro. I examined my thoughts and actions regarding race, and I was honestly shocked at what the examination revealed. Like most other Southerners, I had not been conscious of any moral guilt in my racial attitudes. Like them too, I had taken segregation for granted without bothering to inquire into its underlying implications. But once having understood these implications I could follow only one course. I had to withdraw my approval of the system of white supremacy. I had also to part with many Southern traditions."[1]

And in part he did. In 1945, he entered the Institute of Social Sciences at St. Louis University, by that time an integrated school. Twomey gained a second master's degree, this one in economics. He returned to the South to enter the struggle for interracial justice and for the improvement of the status of the worker. He felt an instinctive identification with the working class. He talked to them often. He listened to them as often as he listened to anyone else. But that wasn't much. He was an exhorter by instinct, not a listener. But he knew people's thwarted hopes. He renewed those hopes.

Ray Ariatti, a labor union business agent who was to join Father Twomey's staff at the Loyola University Institute of Human Relations in 1960, recalls a typical Twomey story. The Jesuit spent his time at a national convention talking to rank-and-file union men. One of them said, "Father, you ought to be talking to the big shots."

"Let me tell you something," Father Twomey responded indignantly. "You are as important as any man in this place. And don't forget it."[2]

Father Twomey set as his goal: "to create a society in which the dignity of the human person in whomsoever found will be acknowledged, respected and protected."[3]

A Jesuit Provincial of the South who, earlier in his career, had assisted Father Twomey, gave this opinion of his work: "He did his greatest work here at Loyola in the Institute of Human Relations and the Institute of Industrial Relations during the last twenty-two years of his life. These institutions enshrined his dream of making a better life for the children of God, his dream of making sure that every man—no matter what his station in life or what his color—was treated as befitted the dignity of creatures stamped with the image of God."[4]

A Southern sociologist-editor who visited Catholic high schools from Texas through Virginia during the early fifties gave a different evaluation. He said that he found, to his amazement, a positive approach to racial questions common to most student leaders at these high schools. He investigated and traced this fresh thinking to talks and seminars presented by Father Twomey at the Summer Schools of Catholic Action.[5]

The Summer Schools of Catholic Action, incidentally, was a youth leadership training week begun by Father Daniel Lord, the National Sodality promoter, in the mid-thirties. It spread throughout the nation so that in the forties, fifties, and sixties, the staff would hold weekly sessions at eight or nine sites throughout the nation. Usually two of these were in the South: one in the Southeast, at Hendersonville, North Carolina, and another in one of the principal cities of Texas. On several occasions, Jackson, Mississippi and New Orleans hosted the sessions. From their beginning, before the Warren Decision, all of these schools had integrated student bodies. The SSCAs, in fact, pioneered integration in many Southern cities such as New Orleans, and in border cities such as St. Louis. At the end of one Summer School of Catholic Action in Houston, a young Texas lady remarked: "Only one thing was wrong with this week. We Southerners should not have been allowed an elective at the time of Father Twomey's interracial talk. Most of us went to it. All of us should have gone. Some of us were racists last Monday. Thank God we are not now."[6]

With his sea captain's voice coming in over the "waves," Twomey expounded ideas on social justice for twenty years to audiences of all kinds in all sections of the nation. He spoke similarly to all, young and old, Northern and Southern, white and black, Catholic and Protestant, expert and amateur. Sometimes his words seemed automatic recordings triggered by such a word as "communism" or "race" or "unionism"—whether in a formal address or in a friendly conversation. Occasionally, a fellow warrior in the fight for social justice would have to say: "Halt, Lou! You don't have to convince me!"

Some might say that he was not a great orator, that none of his speeches will go down in the books of outstanding American speeches, that he did not leave a quotable phrase the Southland remembers. But certainly his total impact hit home. A graduate student in the prestigious department of speech at Louisiana State University, Ann Marie Richard, wrote her master's thesis on the five "Christian in Action" talks Twomey gave over ABC on the five Sundays in June 1958. She called her study "A Rhetorical Analysis of the June 1958 Radio Speeches of Louis J. Twomey."

"Father Twomey's delivery of the addresses," Miss Richard wrote, "was characterized by a strong, deliberate, and articulate voice that radiated warmth and sincerity. His style was almost poetic. He made use of clear expressions and vivid images which gave meaning and vitality to abstract concepts. In addition to amplifying major ideas, his use of parallelism and a triplet linking of concepts in a series reflected a certain rhythm in his oral style."[7]

This series, his greatest effort at presenting his beliefs to the nation at large, deserves careful appraisal. In June 1958, four years after the Warren Decision, when the South had as yet done

83

little to carry out the judgment of the Court, the National Council of Catholic Men invited Father Twomey to give a series of five talks on the ABC network. Martin Work, Executive Director of the NCCM, admitted that most of the "Christian in Action" programs handled devotional, theological or historical topics. But he was not adverse to discussions of the controversial race question. Father Twomey recognized the "terrifying challenge" and "grand opportunity" of speaking on the subject of race over a national hookup."[8] He entitled his speeches "The Race Problem: Basis of World Conflict," "To be Treated Like a Man," "The Hurt in Their Hearts," "In All Fairness," and "Go and Do in Like Manner."[9]

In his first speech he referred extensively to his own Southern background—a double necessity because of his lack of an accent and his unusual attitudes. He understood the motives and psychology of his audience. He organized his speeches carefully, devoted considerable time to the introduction in each talk, and finished with a restatement of his central theme and a call to action. He appealed to religious, ethical, and patriotic motives. He called on reason and emotion. He showed repeated concern for justice for all citizens at home and for the image of America overseas. The response to these talks was great, and surprisingly, predominantly positive.

He was not a scholarly economist or sociologist by inclination, even though he won an advanced degree in economics at the Institute of Social Sciences at St. Louis University. However, sociologists and economists respected him. At an informal gathering in the home of editor Don Thorman during the American Catholic Sociological Convention at Notre Dame in late December 1958, he and Doctor Thomas R. O'Dea held the center of attention—even though almost all the leading Catholic sociologists in the country took part in the discussion.[10]

He recognized the value of sound scholarly studies and used them. He made few himself. That he could do scholarly work he made clear early in his career. While still in his divinity studies he wrote a well-researched theological article for the February 1938 issue of the *American Ecclesiastical Review* entitled, "The Lenten Fast: Is It an Insupportable Burden?" This article set in motion a chain reaction that brought about major changes in the fasting laws of the American Church.[11]

He wrote extensively for magazines, such as the *Queen's Work* that featured him every month. He co-authored (with myself) a pamphlet *Questions and Answers on Communism* that sold 59,015 copies within two years.[12] He put out the *Blueprint for the South,* a monthly mimeographed sheet of four pages, designed to keep young Jesuits abreast of the American social reform scene. Ultimately it went to interested Jesuits throughout the English-speaking countries and helped to make Father Twomey one of the best-known Jesuits in the world. Late in life, he edited the noteworthy monthly *Social Order.* Presumably none of his editorials or essays will live on in American letters; yet his writings, as his speeches, did their job at the time. They helped to prepare the nation and especially the American South for the changes that were to come.

While he loved the Southland where he was born, and loved especially the city of New Orleans, his headquarters for so many years, Father Twomey did not psychologically identify himself with any part of the nation. He was an American rather than a Southerner, a citizen of the world rather than of a particular country. He seemed to have a similar love for every place and every person. He never mentioned Lee or Jackson, or even Gustave Beauregard. He often spoke of Francis of Assisi or Thomas More, of Leo XIII or Pius XI. Yet he felt deeply any aspersion on his loyalty to the region where God had seen fit to place him.

Louis Twomey rarely mentioned the fact that he had played big league ball with the Washington Senators before he joined the Jesuit Order, even in dealing with young men who might have listened to him more attentively had he done so. His only remembered comment about the big leagues came during an All-Star game. When his favorite ball player, Willie Mays, came to bat, someone asked him how much more difficult it was to catch in the big leagues than in college. Twomey replied that it was much easier in the big leagues. Up there, the catcher usually knew that the pitcher would get the ball fairly close to where he intended to throw it.

Louis Twomey did not walk picket lines, but he taught in labor schools. He preferred reason to confrontation. He protested injustice by working to establish justice, by promoting those institutions and organizations that he thought would create a better society. He talked whenever asked, whatever the audience, all over the western hemisphere. He shared platforms with southern politicians, even those who disagreed with him violently. He might joke in private about how they got their offices. But he respected their positions and presumed their integrity, even when few others did.

He sincerely feared Communism and this brought him ridicule from the extremists at either end of political thought. When, shortly after World II, he suggested that Spain might be the only safe anticommunistic base the United States had on the continent of Europe, a progressive weekly put his words in its "doghouse column." His work against Communism should have endeared him to conservative Southerners. But he differed from them in that he called for a just social order to forestall Communism. Some Christian anticommunist crusades that spent time in denouncing Communist advance and ferreting out Communist conspirators thought they had found one in him, even though he had been fighting Communism long before they came on the scene.

In a short article, "Conservatives and Anti-Communism," William F. Buckley, Jr., devoted a full page to a critique of Father Twomey's brand of anticommunism. Buckley began: *"'We are responsible for Communism!'* roars the Rev. Louis J. Twomey in the October 1961 issue of *Act*. I assume he roared out the words,"* Buckley went on, "because in his script he used both the exclamation point and the italics. . . . 'The Communists have advanced,' Twomey said, 'because of our gross unconcern with gross violations of justice and charity here and abroad.'

"Now I," Buckley continued, "find that statement historically nonsensical . . . It is theologically wrong, historically naive, and strategically suicidal to assume that the forces of communism, like those of the devil, are routed by personal or even corporate acts of justice and love.

"Father Twomey believes, for instance, that the segregation of the Negro in the South is the single greatest encouragement to international communism. I would say that the single greatest encouragement to international communism is the existence of a class of people who can make that kind of statement. . . .

"The Communists would find just as much to criticize in an integrated South as in a segregated South, just as they are finding it as easy to criticize our prodigious trade union movement as to criticize the fledgling thing of thirty years ago."[13]

Buckley saw the destruction of Communism as a goal, and power politics as a most effective weapon against it. Twomey saw a just social order as the goal, and as necessary to its attainment, the destruction of Communism. Twomey based his campaign on the anticommunist *Divini Redemptoris* of Pius XI, in many ways the greatest of the encyclicals. The Holy Father urged men to unmask the Communist conspiracy, to resist Communist advances and to establish a Christian social order. In Father Twomey's view, if Communism would disappear by next Christmas, Christians would still have this last-mentioned supreme task. In William Buckley's view, if social injustice would disappear by next Christmas, men would still have to roll back Communism.

Louis Twomey did not have to fight the local ecclesiastical establishment. He strongly supported Archbishop Rummel in his attempt to improve race relations in the New Orleans area. He was, in fact, so close to the Archbishop that other priests often sought his intervention with the prelate in a specific social program—so strong was the mutual esteem of Archbishop and Jesuit.

He did not have to fight the national political establishment. During his adult years, the men in the White House— Roosevelt, Truman, Eisenhower, Kennedy, and Johnson—were open to social advance. President Eisenhower appointed him to the State Advisory Council of the National Civil Rights Commission. President Johnson appointed him to the National Citizens Committee for Community Relations. Twomey numbered many personal friends of long standing among the nation's economic and political leaders, though none ever bought his silence.

He fought the social establishment—the supporters of an unjust way of life who felt threatened by the "Feds," both in labor questions and in interracial affairs. Late in life, in an occasional public address, he might seem to have forgotten how far northern states had gone in passing legislation that supported labor unions. Once, after hearing Father Twomey speak on labor organizations, a listener commented, "Detroit fought and won these battles thirty years ago." But even at that late date, Father Twomey was describing what was still an accurate picture of most of the South. There, in working for the rural poor, he could find support for a welfare venture according to the old paternalistic, patronizing tradition. But when he tried to organize jointly poor white and poor black farm laborers, the guns would fire on Fort Sumter again.

As if the United States did not have enough problems to tax his zeal, Twomey began a project for Latin America late in life. He did not design his programs for diplomats or intellectuals but for the working class leaders of Central America themselves. He took advantage of the strategic location of New Orleans with relation to the lands of the Caribbean.

The General of the Society of Jesus, Pedro Arrupe, showed a close interest in Father Twomey's work and recommended it as a model to Jesuits working in social apostolates in all parts of the world, especially in developing countries. In 1967, in fact, the Jesuit General invited Father Twomey to Rome to assist in the preparation of a letter on social justice and human relations that Father Arrupe intended to send to Jesuits everywhere in the states.[14] The letter, entitled "The Interracial Apostolate" bears the imprint of Father Louis Twomey throughout. The magazine *America* prophesied that this work would prove Father Twomey's "most lasting single achievement."[15]

With all his vigorous campaigns for social justice and his moving in liberal circles, Father Twomey hewed the line on traditional exercises of piety. He gathered his staff at the Loyola University Institute of Human Relations for a common recitation of the Angelus at noon. Like Pope John he never forgot the prayers of his childhood. He prayed for a safe journey, whether across the city, or across the continent. He was a religiously committed man—and even a casual acquaintance would sense that fact immediately. He prayed and his reflection before God often let him see more clearly than some intellectuals and scholars the real problems of his city, his state, his nation, his world.

In the funeral euology for Father Twomey, Thomas Clancy, Vice President of Loyola of the South, and later Jesuit Provincial, said among other tributes: "Any historian who studies the history of post-World War II America must reckon with the figure of Louis J. Twomey. He was one of the original band of labor priests who had a profound influence on the trade union movement in this country. He saw the tragedy of racism in the South, the nation and the world, and fought it manfully. Through his vast publications and through the literally thousands of letters he wrote to people throughout the world, through the hundreds of visitors he entertained and educated to the ignominies as well as the good points of the South, he was perhaps among the six or seven best known priests in America . . . A humble man of God, always conscious of the divine dimension of human affairs, he achieved secular greatness and became one of the most influential men of his time."[16]

A front-page statement in the *New Orleans Clarion World* a few days later said even more: "One of the great men of the modern era died in New Orleans last week. He was the Rev. Louis J. Twomey, S.J., who lived in personal humility but who was a giant in the battle for human rights."[17]

CHAPTER 10

AMERICAN FREEDOM

John Courtney Murray (1904–1967)

While almost all governments in the world controlled or influenced the religious life of their peoples, the American government began with the proposition that its law-making body could make no law respecting the establishment of religion or prohibiting the free exercise thereof. America was saying, in short, that it would ask for Caesar the things that were Caesar's and would leave to God what belonged to Him.

The country that called itself the "eldest daughter of the Church" would soon enact a "Civil Constitution of the Clergy," carefully regulating the ministry of priests. Spain and Portugal had just expelled one of the largest religious orders and seized all its schools and seminaries. England still pressed a crown of thorns called the "Penal Laws" on Irish Catholics. The Austrian Emperor so meddled in Church affairs that he won the nickname "the Imperial Sacristan." Catholic Poland was about to lose its independence. The United States alone offered freedom to Catholics.

One might have thought that the popes would welcome the one government that openly stated that it would not interfere with religious practice. Instead the popes continued to go out of their way to placate hereditary Catholic monarchs who used or abused the Church according to whim. They regularly ignored the one country that would never confiscate the Church's charitable or educational institutions or expel its dedicated apostles. And after a few decades of slight concern, Rome began to make life difficult for American Catholics with what it called a "Syllabus of Errors." A Catholic was anathema or "cursed" or "excommunicated" if he did not hold for the union of church and state, the predominance of the church in public law, and the refusal of public worship to other religions. This set back the full acceptance of the church in America for a century. It proved a continual embarrassment to American Catholics who asked of the Protestant majority what their church would not accord to Protestants in any place where Catholics were in the majority. Catholic editors throughout the country wasted time and space trying to justify this strange political view.[1]

This theory would seem to give to political leaders the capacity to make a religious decision. Yet Rome never explained what gave Czar Alexander III of Russia or Kaiser Wilhelm I of Germany, or even "good old Franz Joseph of Austria" the capacity to make religious decisions. Yet that is what the church was saying: that these rulers should recognize the Catholic Church as the only true Church—a religious not a political decision. If Franz Joseph decided that his Catholic Church was correct and restricted Protestants, what kept Kaiser Wilhelm I from favoring his fellow Protestants and applauding his Chancellor Bismarck's persecution of Catholics. And wouldn't the Church have to approve Czar Alexander III's restrictions on all but Orthodox Christians?

Had not the Church in its very beginning fought the notion of a state-dominated religion when its martyrs defied Nero, Decius, and Diocletian—all powerful emperors? The popes made reluctant concessions to King Francis I of France in the sixteenth century, lest he try to establish an independent state-church as his neighbor in England, Henry VIII, was doing. After several centuries this reluctant concession to the French king and other monarchs became almost a dogma of faith. No one ever explained what gave a civil ruler the competence to make a religious decision. Yet all rulers of all times presumed to do this until the founding Fathers of America said, not simply out of pure speculative wisdom but for many practical reasons, "religion is not government's sphere."

Thirty years after the *Syllabus*, the enlightened pontiff,

Leo XIII, widely rated the greatest pope since the reforming popes in the sixteenth century, limited his praise of the freedom of the Church in America by insisting that the Church would be better off if it had a preferred place in the Republic. He never explained what divine intervention would give the Fifty-fifth American Congress the wisdom or the capacity to make such a law, even if our Constitution had allowed it.

World War I came and shattered the royal families of Europe, destroyed the empires of the Hapsburgs, Romanoffs, and Hohenzollerns. Communism swept Eastern Europe, and six years of World War II brought unspeakable horrors to the world. Troops of the United States and other Allied Powers freed Italy from Nazi and Fascist tyranny. In the aftermath the new Italian government made a treaty with the United States. By this agreement Italy gave freedom to religious minorities. But clerical Rome still looked on the relations of church and state as if nothing had changed.

A Jesuit on the staff of *Civiltà Cattolica,* Florillus Cavalli, could write in April 1948: "The Roman Catholic Church, convinced, through its divine prerogatives, of being the only true church, must demand the right of freedom for herself alone, because such a right can only be possessed by truth, never by error. As to other religions, the Church will certainly never draw the sword, but she will require that by legitimate means they shall not be allowed to propagate false doctrine. Consequently, in a State where the majority of the people are Catholic, the Church will require that legal existence be denied to error, and that if religious minorities actually exist, they shall have only *de facto* existence, without opportunity to spread their beliefs . . . The Church cannot blush for her own want of tolerance, as she asserts it in principle and applies it in practice."[2]

As a result, when America produced an outstanding theologian, "a formal theological thinker who towered above his fellows,"[3] Rome furtively silenced him. It could not even conceive of "due process." That theologian was John Courtney Murray, S.J.

Had his vocation not turned him to the service of the Church during his pre-college years, he could have been an illustrious ambassador to the Court of St. James, or a senior senator from one of the original states of the Eastern seaboard. With an

M.A. from Boston College in 1927, he was every inch a cosmopolitan intellectual. Tall, erect, with an excellent command of the English language, he combined remarkable theological and philosophical insights in church-state relations with an understanding and appreciation of American political institutions. He sympathized and understood the American Protestant and secularist attitudes and engaged in high-yield interdenominational discussion along with his colleague Gustave Weigel.

Murray recognized early that theological reflection must derive from human experience. Further, he raised theological horizons to include historical, sociological, philosophical, and anthropological insights. He frequently conferred with the outstanding Catholic Church historian in the country, Msgr. John Tracy Ellis, whose writings opened up new ecclesiastical vistas. Murray saw at all times, even when he received little support from ecclesiastical administrators, that theologians could move ahead only in collaboration with the Church's authoritative teachers.

Americans should not take for granted the permanent acceptance by the world-at-large of the tremendous insights he left. European writers have written of the Vatican Council without mentioning his name even in the discussion of religious freedom. They would put supporters of his views on the defensive even today. His entire thought deserves careful attention and constant reflection, but particularly suitable to the purpose of this study, is his attempt to get the Church to take a more positive view of church and state relationships, based on the American experience.

The son of a Scottish lawyer and an Irish mother, both New Yorkers, Murray earned his doctorate in theology at the Gregorian University in Rome in 1937. He taught at Woodstock College, near Baltimore. At the same time, he became religion editor of *America,* the Jesuit weekly magazine, and editor of *Theological Studies*. He did ground-breaking work in ecumenism. Lutheran theologian Martin E. Marty of the University of Chicago rated Murray "first among those whose voice was heard beyond Catholicism."[4]

When Murray began to bring a fresh Atlantic breeze into the stagnant atmosphere of church-state thinking, his chief opponent came from New England, not from the limited confines of dictator-ridden Europe. Msgr. Joseph C. Fenton was editor of the *American Ecclesiastical Review*. Fenton's friend, the Redemptorist Francis J. Connell, supported him. Even more, Fenton could depend on the Holy Office in Rome, whose positions he upheld.

In a cursory meeting with the jovial, rotund Monsignor Fenton, such as a dinner at an Italian restaurant while the music box carried the voice of Enrico Caruso, one could not but enjoy the man's company. He would regale his hearers with stories of Rome or of Cardinal Spellman's late night phone calls to read his latest religious verse.

Murray, on the other hand, more the Scot divine than the typical Irish monsignor, was a formidable person in appearance as in intellectual exchange, not given to casual talk, rarely satisfied with a three-syllable word when he could find one of four syllables, not hesitant to let another know that he probably would not be able to follow Murray's line of thought. Fenton, on the contrary, tried to answer one's objections, even if his argumentation did not ordinarily stand on its own TV tower, without supporting wires connecting it with Rome.

Fenton admitted no area of originality or creativeness in theology. Competence could and would show itself exclusively in clear statement of given doctrine.[5] In Fenton's view, common at the time, the Church had always possessed all the answers. The theologian defended and explained these assumptions. Fenton saw only hostility on the outside—an attitude true perhaps before World War II, but not verified by the experiences of Murray and his colleague, Gustave Weigel, S.J., in ecumenical discussions.

While Fenton circled the theological wagons, Murray looked for jet planes to move beyond the ridges. He would not be satisfied with the practical acceptance of freedom of worship, based on the notion that Catholics had to grant it in predominantly Catholic countries to enjoy it elsewhere. He sought a clear and unqualified statement on religious liberty. "The principle of religious freedom," he was to write, "has long been recognized in constitutional law, to the point where even Marxist-Leninist political ideology is obliged to pay lip service to it. In all honesty it must be admitted that the Church is late in acknowledging the validity of this principle."[6]

Had Murray and Fenton debated the issue publicly on TV

as John F. Kennedy and Vice President Richard M. Nixon were to debate the issues of 1960, Murray would have carried the day. But it was not an open American-type debate. The Roman Curia wanted its position upheld, even if its church-state views rested on quicksand. Msgr. Fenton simply defended the flabby traditional opinion, and when he could not face up to the Murray argumentation, the Holy Office (the old Inquisition with a public relations title) would intervene.

The Curia advised the American Assistant of the Jesuit General, Father Vincent McCormick, S.J., that Father Murray treaded on hot coals. It urged the Superior of the Holy Cross Order in Rome to forestall Murray's appearance on the prestigious campus of Notre Dame University; it set out to force the withdrawal from publication of an important book, published by the University of Notre Dame Press, *The Catholic Church* in *World Affairs* because of Murray's essay on "The Structure of the Church-State Problem."[7]

By July 1955, the "Inquisition" had silenced the greatest of American Catholic theologians. The mood changed when John XXIII became pope. He had a sense of Church history and created an atmosphere wherein the Church dropped many old patterns of thought. He called the Council; and between the first and second session, he issued the encyclical *Pacem in Terris* in 1963. In this message to the whole world—his last, for he was to die soon after—he praised many of the institutions of government that the Free World took for granted: the limitation on the term of the executive, varied opportunities to participate in government, a charter of fundamental rights, a document called the Constitution that determined the respective spheres of government, mutual relationships, and systems, administrators should follow. In paragraph ten of this letter, Pope John came out in support of what Father Murray had long taught: "Every human being has the right to honor God according to the dictates of an upright conscience, and therefore the right to worship God privately and publicly."[8]

John Courtney Murray did not attend the First Session of the Council, but Msgr. Fenton received an invitation. Murray had been "disinvited," to use his exquisite word. Even after Murray came to later sessions of the Council at the invitation of Francis Cardinal Spellman of New York, the Apostolic Delegate to the United States, Archbishop Egidio Vagnozzi, working with the curial conservatives, hounded him for writing an article "On Religious Liberty," in the November 22-30th, 1964 issues of *America* magazine.[9]

Murray sharply questioned Vagnozzi's interference: "He is in no sense an official of the Council."[10] Murray would win; but the opposition continued its petty persecution. The intricate details of the curial maneuverings to table the discussion of religious liberty at the third session of the Council and the reaction of a large group of bishops led by Albert Cardinal Meyer of Chicago, belong to the general history of the Council rather than specifically to the efforts of John Courtney Murray in trying to return the Church to its ancient position as protector of freedom.

Pope Paul VI, who had reconvened the Second Vatican Council a few months after John XXIII's death, put his name to the Declaration of Religious Liberty, December 7, 1965. It was the single conciliar document addressed to the entire world.[11] The Council ended the following day. John Courtney Murray summarized the document: "Its content is properly doctrinal. In particular three doctrinal tenets are declared: the ethical doctrine of religious freedom as a human right (personal and collective); a political doctrine with regard to the functions and limits of government in matters religious; and the theological doctrine of the freedom of the Church as the fundamental principle in what concerns the relations between the Church and the socio-political order."[12]

The Council lifted the biggest burden that weighed down the shoulders of American Catholics in their dealings with their separated brethren. And for once, a priest who had fought the establishment had won.

When in the fourth session of the Council, United States bishops rose to speak in defense of the Declaration of Religious Liberty, drafted in great part by Murray, one of them commented to Bishop Robert E. Tracy of Baton Rouge, Louisiana, "The voices are the voices of the United States bishops; but the thoughts are the thoughts of John Courtney Murray."[13]

EPILOGUE

What did the rebelling or reforming priests accomplish? Collectively they attained little; individually, little or much depending on the individual or the cause. They were such diverse personalities and worked for such isolated causes that even those contemporary to each other, like McGlynn and O'Leary, had little combined impact. Had either of them, for instance, served under James Cardinal Gibbons in Baltimore, a man far more sympathetic to their purposes, they might have had little cause to rebel. This points out a lack in the diocesan structure. As members of religious orders, the Markoe brothers could find another assignment with honor. Diocesan priests, who fall out with their bishops, find it more difficult to do that.

The fact that the reforming priests had no single impact stemmed in part from two aspects of church structure. The priests had no independent association to allow them to stand together or to assist a blacklisted brother. The various dioceses still have no provision for a constructive minority in the formation of policy. With no machinery to support holders of minority points of view, each rebel priest stood publicly alone, seemingly an oddball outside the fold, a maverick or troublemaker, while in actuality many other priests and laymen often sided with their views.

Further, each rebel priest had his own area of interest, his own way of protest, his own answers to basic questions. They were diverse personality types. Cummings would have avoided conflicts had not events thrust him into one. O'Leary would have sought war even in peaceful times. Theobald was a scholar by inclination; Markoe an activist, with little sympathy for scholarship; McGlynn was the distinguished pastor of one of the largest parishes in America's largest city; Cummings, an obscure shepherd in out-of-the-way places; Twomey, a kindly concilia tory man by inclination, never spoiled for a fight, and never backed away from one; the belligerent O'Leary went out looking for battle. A single event put Cummings in the limelight; Ryan stood in the public gaze all his adult life. McGlynn had one basic concern, poverty, and one main answer; Twomey fought on a wide front—race, labor, inter-American affairs—and offered many answers to all issues involved. Murray focused on one issue: freedom.

Some of the things they fought for became a part of American life. The workingmen have a far more secure place in American society than when John Augustine Ryan walked into town from the Minnesota prairies. The blacks moved forward remarkably between the ordination of Stephen Theobald and the death of William Markoe. Cornelius O'Leary and Edward McGlynn effected little directly, but their concern for the workingman influenced Cardinal Gibbons, and through him, the Roman authorities, in the interests of organized labor. The memory of Edward McGlynn alerts us to the fact that even today the church in America needs "due process" and public, impartial judgment.

Some men will have to bear witness regularly in dramatic, even perhaps bizarre ways, to society's failures. Others may urge them to "let well enough alone," or warn them not "to rock the boat," or mock their objectives with other cliches of caution. The defenders of the status quo may even launch their criticism of the rebel by identifying themselves with the New Testament or by evoking the image of Plymouth Rock. But no offensive can cloud the fact that rebels have many functions. One of these is to alert society to possibilities for improvement.

Each of the reformers discussed in this book had something in common with the legendary Swiss hero Arnold Von Wienkelried. Von Wienkelried is remembered for having gathered into his own chest the Austrian spears, so that the wedge of

Swiss infantry could pierce the otherwise impregnable Austrian battle line. The reforming priests were also willing to take their share of "spears" so that those who followed were able to break through the solid wall in front of them.

Each of the rebel or reforming priests had his quirks, his little inconsistencies, his occasional high-handedness. He may even have "played to the crowd" on occasion or sought publicity for its own sake, or delighted in disturbing the "sensibilities of squares." An observer might have said, "If only he had done this . . . ." Or, "Had he heen more prudent in that . . . . ." But those distinctive qualities helped to make him what he was. Had he had greater prudence, more reserve, greater flexibility and willingness to compromise, he might have accommodated himself to the establishment or even served it as an acquiescent member of society.

If not always responding in a way others might have liked, still each of these men obeyed a call to action. Only the New Testament expresses how best to judge their lives. "By their fruits you shall know them." Isn't the world a better place because they worked, each in his own way, to make it better?

NOTES

INTRODUCTION

1. Albert S. Foley, S.J., tells the confusing story of his publishing experiences in an article entitled "Adventures in Black Catholic History: Research and Writing," in the *U.S. Catholic Historian*, vol. 5, 1(1986):103–18.

One archbishop encouraged him to research and write his potentially most influential work, *The Catholic Church and the Washington Negro*, and then ordered the withdrawal of the book's *imprimatur* after the University of North Carolina Press had considered the book for publication (p. 105). Another archbishop, also a Cardinal, used his influence to have his book *Bishop Healy: Beloved Outcaste* published (pp. 114–15).

CHAPTER 1: PATRIOT PRIEST OF THE WEST

1. Sister Angelita Myerscough, A.S.C., Master's thesis, "Pierre Gibault, Missionary Priest" (St. Louis University, 1947). Father Joseph P. Donnelly, S. J. *Pierre Gibault, Missionary, 1737–1802* (Chicago: Loyola University Press, 1971) remains the authoritative biography.

2. Gibault to Briand, Dec. 4, 1775. The text of this letter appears in the Records of the American Catholic Historical Association of Philadelphia, 20(1909):423–24.

3. Gibault to Briand, June 15, 1769, in the Illinois State Historical Collections, (hereafter IHC), 16:560.

4. Meurin to Briand, June 14, 1769, in IHC, 16:549.

5. Gibault to Briand, June 20, 1772, in the Archives of the Archdiocese of Quebec (hereafter AAQ), E.U., 6:28.

6. Meurin to Briad, May 23, 1776, in AAQ, E.U., 6:42.

7. Donnelly, 76–77.

8. Ibid., 71–72.

9. Gibault to Briand, May 22, 1789, in IHC, 5:585.

CHAPTER 2: CONFEDERATE AGENT

1. *New Catholic Encyclopedia*, 2:52–3.

2. *Dublin Telegraph*, July 14, 1913.

3. *St. Louis Republic*, Aug. 1, 1913.

4. Ibid.

5. Ibid.

6. *Bannon's Diary*, 1862–3, in the Yates Snowden Collection, South Caroliniana Library, University of South Carolina, Columbia.

7. Bannon to Snowden, Dublin, Feb. 20, 1905, loc. cit.

8. Benjamin to Mason, Richmond, July 6, 1863, Pickett Papers, Library of Congress, Division of Manuscripts.

9. Benjamin to Capston, Richmond, July 3, 1863, Pickett Papers, loc. cit.

10. Bannon to Snowden, Dublin, Feb. 20, 1905, Pickett Papers, loc. cit.

11. Ibid.

12. Bannon to Benjamin, Dec. 15, 1863, with enclosure. Pickett Papers, loc. cit.

13. Bannon to Benjamin, Dublin, Nov. 22, 1863, in Pickett Papers, loc. cit.

14. Bannon to Benjamin, Dublin, Feb. 17, 1864, in Pickett Papers, loc. cit.

15. Bannon Lecture Tour, Mar. 9, 1864, in Pickett Papers, loc. cit.

16. Albert C. Danner, "Father Bannon's Secret Mission," in the *Confederate Veteran*, 27 (1919):180.

17. William M. Leftwich, *Martyrdom in Missouri*, 2 vols., St. Louis, S. W. Book and Publishing Co., 1870.

CHAPTER 3: THE IRONCLAD OATH

1. Records, Calvary Cemetery, St. Louis, June 10, 1873.

2. Records, St. Vincent's Hospital, St. Louis, June 1873.

3. *St. Louis Dispatch*, October 30, 1865.

4. Walter Williams and Floyd Calvin Shoemaker, *Missouri, Mother of the West*, New York: The American Historical Society, 1930, 109.

5. Francis M. Thorpe, Ed., *American Charters, Constitutions, and Organic Laws,* Washington, 1909, 2178.

6. Constitution of Missouri, 1865, Article 2, Section 3.

7. P. R. Kenrick to J. B. Goeldin, Archives of the Archdiocese of St. Louis, July 1865. The *Missouri Republican* published an English translation of this letter, July 30, 1865.

8. Ibid.

9. See *Bates Diary,* July 18, 1865, 218, Missouri Historical Society, St. Louis.

10. Circuit Court Records, Pike County, Missouri, vol. 1; see also T. J. C. Fagg, *Reminiscences,* manuscript, Missouri Historical Society, passim.

11. John Hogan, *On the Mission in Missouri,* Kansas City, 1892, 128–32.

12. *Missouri Republican,* September 21, 1865.

13. Ibid.

14. Ibid.

15. William Leftwich, *Martyrdom in Missouri,* St. Louis, vol. 2:343.

16. *Missouri Republican,* September 12, 1865.

17. Records of the County Court, Pike County, vol. 1.

18. *St. Louis Republic,* March 5, 1892.

19. *New York Observer,* September 28, 1865, reprinted in *Missouri Republican,* October 3, 1865.

20. Kenrick to Miller, September 15, 1865; printed in *St. Louis Republic,* March 8, 1896, at the death of Kenrick.

21. *True Flag,* Louisiana, Missouri, September 23, 1865.

22. *Missouri Republican,* September 22, 1865.

23. Ibid., October 19 and 26, 1865; *St. Louis Dispatch,* October 17, 1865.

24. Francis P. Blair, Jr. to M. Blair, November 4, 1865, *Blair Papers,* Manuscripts Division, Library of Congress.

25. Ibid.

26. David D. Field, *Speeches, Arguments and Miscellaneous Papers,* A. P. Sprague, ed. New York: Appleton and Company, 1884, p. 100. For a more complete view of the legal aspects of this case see Harold C. Bradley, "In Defense of John Cummings," in *Missouri Historical Review,* LVIII (October 1962), pp. 10–15. In a chapter entitled "Radical Vindictiveness," chapter 4 of *Missouri Under Radical Rule, 1865–1870* (Columbia, MO: University of Missouri Press, 1865), 65–75, William E. Parrish discusses the case of Father Cummings in the light of Missouri history of the time.

27. Garner et al. vs. Board of Public Works of Los Angeles, et al., 341 United States (1952):716–30.

CHAPTER 4: THE KNIGHTS OF LABOR

1. John Rothensteiner, *History of the Archdiocese of St. Louis* (St. Louis: Blackwell Wielandy, Co., 1928), 2:526.

2. Henry J. Browne, *The Catholic Church and the Knights of Labor* (Washington: The Catholic University of America Press, 1949), 158ff., 222, 280–81.

3. *St. Louis Globe-Democrat,* Jan. 3, 4, 8, 16, 1878.

4. Browne, 108–9.

5. John Tracy Ellis, *The Life of Cardinal Gibbons,* 2 vols. (Milwaukee: Bruce Publishing Co., 1952), 1:495–97.

6. *Globe-Democrat,* May 13, 1886.

7. *St. Louis Post-Dispatch,* April 2, 1886.

8. *Globe-Democrat,* April 2, 1886.

9. *O'Leary to Powderly,* De Soto, September 20, 1886, in *Powderly Papers* in the Mullen Library, The Catholic University of America, Washington, D.C.

10. *Post-Dispatch,* April 3, April 9, 1886.

11. U.S. Congress, House, *Investigation of Labor Troubles in Missouri, Arkansas, Kansas, Texas and Illinois,* House of Representatives Report 4174, 49th Congress, 2d sess., 1887, pp. 468–69.

12. House Report, 4174, pp. 470–72.

13. *Post-Dispatch,* April 7, 1886.

14. Records of St. Rose of Lima's Church, De Soto, Missouri.

15. *Western Watchman,* September 4, 1886.

16. O'Leary to Powderly, St. Louis, April 4, 1887, in *Powderly Papers.*

17. *Connecticut Catholic,* November 20, 1886.

18. Browne, 222.

19. Powderly to O'Leary, Scranton, September 27, 1886, in *Powderly Papers.*

20. O'Leary to Powderly, De Soto, October 1886 in *Powderly Papers.*

21. Ibid.

22. Ryan to Corrigan, Philadelphia, April 21, 1886, in *Archives of the Archdiocese of New York.*

23. Browne, 217.

24. *Western Watchman,* September 11, 1886.

25. O'Leary to Powderly, January 23, 1877, in *Powderly Papers.* O'Leary heard the story of the Kenrick-Hoxie meeting from Father John J. Hennessey, Pastor of St. John's Church in St. Louis, where Kenrick resided at

the time. Hennessey was to become bishop of Wichita in 1889 (O'Leary to Powderly, March 30, 1887, in *Powderly Papers*).

26. Browne, p. 212.

27. O'Leary to Powderly, January 23, 1877, in *Powderly Papers*.

28. Records of St. Rose of Lima parish, De Soto, Missouri, p. 379.

29. "A McGlynn Case in Saint Louis," *New York Sun*, April 5, 1887.

30. Powderly to O'Leary, Scranton, April 6, 1887, in *Powderly Papers*.

31. Powderly to Gibbons, June 30, 1887, in Baltimore Archdiocese Archives, 82-W-9.

32. Ibid.

33. Ellis, *Life of Cardinal Gibbons*, 1:521–24.

34. *Globe-Democrat*, October 4, 1887.

35. O'Leary to Powderly, St. Louis, June 4, 1888, in *Powderly Papers*.

36. Terence V. Powderly, *The Path I Trod*, ed. by Harry J. Carman, et al. (New York, 1940), 380.

CHAPTER 5: THE WAR ON POVERTY

1. *New York Sun*, April 30, 1870.

2. John Tracy Ellis, *The Life of James Cardinal Gibbons*, 1:550. I have relied extensively in this chapter on the remarkable research and analysis of Monsignor Ellis in this outstanding work, especially chapter 13, "The Case of Henry George and Dr. McGlynn." All the Baltimore and New York archival references stem from this book. He has left all Church historians in his debt.

3. Frederick J. Zwierlein, *Life and Letters of Bishop McQuaid* (Rochester, 1925–27) 3:7–11.

4. Stephen Bell, *Rebel Priest and Prophet*, New York, 1937, p. 135.

5. Ellis, op. cit., 1:595.

6. Moore to Gibbons, St. Augustine, January 15, 1887, in the Baltimore Cathedral Archives (hereafter BCA) 82-L-10. Ellis cites all the materials taken from the Baltimore Cathedral Archives; op cit., passim.

7. Burtsell *Letter Book*, Account of Interview with Gibbons, January 28, 1887, pp. 332–38, in New York Archdiocesan Archives.

8. Gibbons to Corrigan, Rome, February 18, 1887, Personal, in BCA.

9. Gibbons to Burtsell, Rome, February 18, 1887, Copy, pp. 2–3, in Burtsell *Letter Book*, loc. cit.

10. Gibbons to Simeoni, Rome, February 25, 1887, unclassified, in BCA.

11. Ellis, op. cit., 1:559.

12. Corrigan to Gibbons, New York, April 12, 1887, 82-P-12, in BCA.

13. Bell, op. cit., 133.

14. Speech published in the *Standard,* and quoted in Bell, op. cit., p. 134.

15. Ellis, op. cit., 1:562.

16. *Baltimore Sun,* September 12, 1887.

17. Elder to Gibbons, Cincinnati, July 11, 1887, 83-B-5, in BCA.

18. Edward McGlynn, "The New Know-Nothingism and the Old," in *The North American Review,* 165 (August 1887):195.

19. Ibid., 198.

20. Ibid., 201.

21. Ibid., 201–2.

22. Ibid., 202.

23. Ibid.

24. Dennis O'Connell to Gibbons, Rome, August 1, 1893, 91-R-1, in BCA.

25. *Forum,* 22 (February 1897):695–705.

26. McGlynn to Gibbons, Newburg, May 21, 1897, BCA.

27. Ellis, op. cit., 1:594.

28. Quoted in Bell, op. cit., 280.

CHAPTER 6: BLACK PROTÉGÉ OF A FIGHTING ARCHBISHOP

1. A fine short sketch of Father Stephen Theobald is Albert Sidney Foley's "The Fighting Archbishop's Protégé," Chapter X of *God's Men of Color* (New York: Farrar, Straus & Co., 1955), 95–103.

2. Quoted, ibid., 96.

3. Ibid., 97.

4. *The Chronicle,* 4, 11(November 1931):656.

5. Miriam T. Murphy, "Catholic Missionary Work Among the Colored People of the United States, 1776–1866," in Records of the American Catholic Historical Society, 35, 2 (June 1924):101–36 (hereafter Records).

6. Stephen L. Theobald, "Catholic Missionary Work Among the Colored People of the United States, 1776–1866," in Records, 35, 4(December 1924):325–44.

7. Ibid., 328.

8. Ibid., 331.

9. Ibid., 338.

10. Ibid.

11. Ibid., 332.

12. Ibid., 339.

13. Ibid., 343.

14. Stephen L. Theobald, "Our Heroes and Aspirations," in *The Chronicle*, 4, 11(November 1931):657.

15. Ibid.

16. Ibid., 658–59.

CHAPTER 7: SOUND SOCIAL LEGISLATION

1. John A. Ryan, "A Program of Social Reform by Legislation," in *The Catholic World*, July-Aug. 1909, 433–44; 608–14.

2. Report of the Joint Legislative Committee Investigating Seditious Activities, April 24, 1929, State Senate of New York, 1:1139.

3. Privileged Sources.

4. Francis J. Broderick, S.J., *Rt. Rev. New Dealer, John A. Ryan* (New York: Macmillan Co., 1963) 140.

CHAPTER 8: A SEGREGATED CITY

1. William Markoe, "Autobiography," " (unpublished manuscript) in the Missouri Jesuit Province Archives, 22–24.

2. Ibid., 29.

3. 34 ff.

4. Markoe, "The Importance of Negro Leadership," in *America*, XXIX, 26 (Oct. 13, 1923): 605–606; also "Negro Higher Education," XXVI, 2 (Apr. 1, 1922): 558–60.

5. Markoe, "The Negro and Catholicism," Ibid., XXX, 19, (Feb. 23, 1924): 449–450; "A Great Migration," XXX, 17, (Feb. 9, 1924): 396–7.

6. John J. Albert, S.S.J., "The Negro Leader and the Church," in *America*, XXX, 21 (Mar. 8, 1924): 497–8.

7. Sister Georgianna Rockwell, S.B.S. *Finding Christ in the Ghetto: The Child Converts of St. Nicholas School*, monograph pp. 14–15; an interview with Sister M. Praxedes Wachter, S.B.S., Feb. 20 and Feb. 22, 1980, Ibid., 17–19.

8. Daniel T. Kelleher, "St. Louis 1916 Residential Segregation Ordinance," in the *Bulletin* of the Missouri Historical Society, 26, 3 (April 1970): 245–46.

9. Glennon to Fumasoni-Biondi, St. Louis, Feb. 18, 1927, in St. Louis Archdiocesan Archives.

10. Ibid.

11. Markoe, op. cit., 91.

12. Ibid.

13. Ibid., 96.

14. Ibid., 140.

15. *St. Elizabeth's Chronicle,* 1, 1(January 1928).

16. Ibid., 3, 1(January 1930):1.

17. Ibid.

18. Ibid., passim.

19. Stephen Theobald, "Our Heroes and Aspirations," in *The Chronicle,* 4, 11 (November 1931): 658.

20. *Interracial Review,* 5, 11(November 1932).

21. Ibid., 6, 1(January 1933):12–13.

22. Ibid., 7, 8(September 1934):106.

23. John La Farge, *The Manner Is Ordinary* (New York: Harcourt, Brace and Co., 1954) 339.

24. John T. White, "Survey of Organized Catholic Activities Among the Negroes in the St. Louis District, 1919–1937." Master's thesis, St. Louis University, 1937, 2.

25. Ibid., passim.

26. Markoe, op. cit., 396–99.

27. William B. Faherty, S.J. and Madeline Oliver, *The Religious Roots of Black Catholics in St. Louis* (Florissant, Mo., St. Stanislaus Museum, 1977), *passim.*

CHAPTER 9: SOCIAL JUSTICE IN THE SOUTH

1. Louis J. Twomey, "The Race Problem: Basis of World Conflict," in *Christian in Action* Series, June 1, 1958 (Washington: NCCM, 1958) 1.

2. Mel Leavitt, "Jesuit Was Giant Human Rights Leader," in *New Orleans Clarion Herald,* October 16, 1969, Sect. 2, p. 4.

3. Dale Curry, "Warrior for Human Dignity," in *Men of the South,* vol. 33, 4(August 1969):3.

4. Thomas Clancy, S.J., "Funeral Sermon for Louis Twomey," in *Blueprint,* 22, 2(October 1969):2.

5. Interview with R. E. Bernard, October 15, 1959.

6. My recollections of the occasion.

7. Ann Marie Richard, *A Rhetorical Analysis of the June 1958 Radio Speeches of Louis J. Twomey* (Master's thesis, Louisiana State University, 1971), 139.

8. Twomey to Work, April 24, 1958, quoted in Richard, op. cit., 35.

9. Richard, op. cit., 39.

10. My own recollections.

11. Louis J. Twomey, S.J., "The Lenten Fast: Is It an Insupportable Burden?" in the *American Ecclesiastical Review*, 11, 2(February 1938):97–110.

12. In the Records of the Queen's Work Publishing Company, St. Louis, Mo.

13. William F. Buckley, Jr., "Conservatives and Anti-Communism," in *Ave Maria*, April 7, 1962, 7.

14. *Clarion Herald*, October 16, 1969, 6.

15. *America*, October 25, 1969, 349.

16. Clancy, op. cit., 2.

17. *Clarion World*, October 16, 1969, 1.

CHAPTER 10: AMERICAN FREEDOM

1. John Gilmary Shea, *The Catholic Church in the United States* (New York: Shea, 1892), 4:607–08.

2. Florillus Cavalli, "La Condizione dei Protestanti in Spagna," in *La Civilta Cattolica*, 2(April 1948):29–47.

3. Martin E. Marty, "Foreword," to Donald E. Pelotte, S.S.S., *John Courtney Murray, Theologian in Conflict* (New York: The Paulist Press, 1975), ix.

4. Ibid.

5. *American Ecclesiastical Review*, 134 (January 1956):24–36.

6. John Courtney Murray, "Religious Freedom," in *The Documents of Vatican II*, edited by Walter Abott, S.J. (New York: The Guild Press, 1966), 673.

7. Pelotte, p. 49. I was on the staff of the *Queen's Work Magazine* in St. Louis when an early review copy of the book was delivered there. I recall the circumstances of the time as Pelotte recounts them.

8. John XXIII, *Pacem in Terris*, passim, Rome, 1963.

9. John J. McGinty, to Murray, February 26, 1964, Woodstock College Archives.

10. Murray to McGinty, May 16, 1964, Woodstock College Archives.

11. Franklin H. Littell, in Abbott, 699.

12. Murray, in Abbott, 672–73.

13. Bishop Robert E. Tracy, *American Bishop at the Vatican Council* (New York: McGraw Hill Book Co., 1966), 172.

RECOMMENDED READING

CHAPTER 1: REV. PIERRE GIBAULT

Donnelly, Rev. Joseph P. *Pierre Gibault: Missionary 1732-1802.* Chicago: Loyola University Press, 1971. "Pierre Gibault and the Critical Period of the Illinois Country, 1768-78," 81-82. McDermott, John Francis, ed. *The French in the Mississippi Valley.* Urbana: University of Illinois Press, 1965.

New Catholic Encyclopedia, s.v. "Pierre Gibault."

CHAPTER 2: REV. JOHN B. BANNON

Historical Records and Studies of the United States Historical Society, 1936 s.v. "Father John Bannon," 26:92-98; "Confederate Agents in Ireland," 26:68-88.

New Catholic Encyclopedia, s.v. "John B. Bannon."

CHAPTER 3: REV. JOHN A. CUMMINGS

Bradley, Harold C. "John A. Cummings and the Missouri Test Oath, 1865." Master's thesis, St. Louis University, 1965.

———. "In defense of John Cummings." In *Missouri Historical Review* 58(October 1962):10-15.

Faherty, Rev. William B. "American Hero Anonymous: John Cummings and the Ironclad Oath." In *St. Louis Bar Journal* 27 4(Spring 1981):56-58.

CHAPTER 4: REV. CORNELIUS O'LEARY

Faherty, Rev. William B. "The Clergyman and Labor Progress: Cornelius O'Leary and the Knights of Labor," in *Labor History*. Vol. 2 2(Spring 1970):175-89.
Smith, Mary Constance. In *Our Pastors in Calvary*, 140-41. St. Louis, 1924.

CHAPTER 5: REV. EDWARD MCGLYNN

Bell, Stephen Bell. *Rebel Priest and Prophet*. New York, 1937.
Dictionary of American Biography. s.v. "Edward McGlynn." Written by Msgr. John A. Ryan.
Ellis, Rev. John Tracy. *The Life of James Cardinal Gibbons, Archbishop of Baltimore, 1834-1921*. Ch. 13, "The Case of Henry George and Doctor McGlynn," 1:547-94. Milwaukee: Bruce Publishing Co., 1952.

CHAPTER 6: REV. STEPHEN THEOBALD

Foley, Albert Sidney. *God's Men of Color*. Ch. 10, "The Fighting Archbishop's Protégé." Farrar, Straus and Co., 1955.

CHAPTER 7: REV. JOHN A. RYAN

Broderick, Francis J. *Rt. Rev. New Dealer, Msgr. John A. Ryan*, New York: Macmillan, 1963.
Ryan, Rev. John A. *Social Doctrine in Action*. New York: Harper & Brothers Publishers, 1941.

CHAPTER 8: REV. WILLIAM MARKOE

Markoe, Rev. William. "Memoirs." Archives of Missouri Jesuit Province.
Nickels, Marilyn W. "The Federated Colored Catholics: A Study of Three Variant Perspectives on Racial Justice as Represented by John La Farge, William Markoe, and Thomas Turner." Ph.D. dissertation. Washington: Catholic University of America, 1975. Dr. Nickels is not as sympathetic to Markoe as to the other two men.

CHAPTER 9: REV. LOUIS TWOMEY

Curry, Dale, "Warrior for Human Dignity," in Clarion Herald (New Orleans), October 16, 1969. *Men of the South,* vol. 33, no. 4(August 1969):3. Loyola University of New Orleans.

Richard, Ann Marie. "A Historical Analysis of the June 1958 Radio Speeches of Louis J. Twomey. Master's thesis: Louisiana State University, 1971.

CHAPTER 10: REV. JOHN COURTNEY MURRAY

Pelotte, S.S.S., Rev. Donald E. *John Courtney Murray, Theologian in Conflict.* New York: Paulist Press, 1975.

Index